TIANANMEN:
THE RAPE OF PEKING

TIANANMEN

THE RAPE OF PEKING

Michael Fathers and Andrew Higgins
Edited by Robert Cottrell

THE INDEPENDENT

THE INDEPENDENT in association with DOUBLEDAY

London NewYork Toronto Sydney Auckland

THE INDEPENDENT
Newspaper Publishing plc,
40 City Road,
London EC1Y 2DB

TRANSWORLD PUBLISHERS LTD
61-63 Uxbridge Road, London W5 5SA

TRANSWORLD PUBLISHERS (AUSTRALIA) PTY LTD
15-23 Helles Avenue, Moorebank, NSW 2170

TRANSWORLD PUBLISHERS (NZ) LTD
Cnr Moselle and Waipareira Aves, Henderson,Auckland

DOUBLEDAY CANADA LTD
105 Bond Street, Toronto, Ontario M5B 1Y3

Published 1989 by The Independent in association with Doubleday
a division of Transworld Publishers Ltd
Copyright © 1989 Newspaper Publishing plc, Michael Fathers,
Andrew Higgins and Robert Cottrell

British Library Cataloguing in Publication Data

Fathers, Michael, *1941 –*
    Tiananmen: The rape of Peking
    1. China. Peking. Political events
    I. Title II. Higgins, Andrew, *1958 – III.* Cottrell, Robert
    951'.156058
    ISBN 0-385-40022-5

Printed by Jarrold Printing, Norwich

CONTENTS

MICHAEL FATHERS, 48, was born in New Zealand, and served with the New Zealand Press Association in Wellington. He joined Reuters in 1969, and was posted to Vietnam, Cambodia, Afghanistan, Pakistan, Thailand, Burma and Singapore. In 1986, he came to the *The Independent* as Asia Editor. He is married with two children, and lives in London.

ANDREW HIGGINS, 31, has been Peking correspondent of *The Independent* since 1987. After reading Chinese at Cambridge University, he spent a post-graduate year at Shandong University, China. His first job was as a translator for the United States consulate in Hong Kong. In 1982, he joined Reuters, and served postings in Nairobi and Paris.

ACKNOWLEDGEMENTS

This book was made possible only by the assistance and encouragement of many people and departments within *The Independent*. It is a product of the newspaper as much as of the authors.

Vivienne Conlon undertook the management of this book; Lucy Taylor, the production; Linda Tanner, the publicity; Bernard Higton, the design; and Alex Maxey, the sub-editing. Their kindness, enthusiasm and attention to detail set standards which we, as authors, were hard-pushed to match.

Our thanks are due to the *Independent* foreign desk, headed by Nick Ashford, which absorbed the absence of three staff with disconcerting ease; the library, under Justin Arundale, for the cheerful omniscience with which it responded to an exceptional and unexpected volume of research requests; the operations department, for constructing a word-processing network smart enough to have written the book by itself; Frances Cutler and Sarah Heneghan on the picture desk, for the succession of startling images displayed on later pages; Pam Williams for her many hours spent reproducing the colour pictures; and the art department — William Bown, Robert Brooks, Kristina Ferris and Ciárán Hughes — for its grace and patience. Kevin Hamlin in Hong Kong, Peter Pringle in Washington and Tim McGirk in Madrid devoted exceptional amounts of time and effort to uncovering sources and materials on our behalf.

Most of all, we have depended upon our researchers, Jane Duckett and Tina Tong. They established with formidable speed the indexes upon which we drew; they translated, checked, filed, retrieved, sought, found, read and re-checked with awesome dedication.

We have talked to many people who were with us in Peking during this period. Wuerkaixi, Seth Faison, Adi Ignatius, Xiao Yi, Dorinda Elliott, Tim Luard, James Miles, Robert Thomson, John Pomfret, Jane Macartney, Joseph Kahn and Vivica Abrahams, we are happy to salute here by name. Others, whom at their own request we do not identify, we also thank warmly.

Finally, we are indebted to our families and close friends. May the completion of this book serve as some modest compensation for the strains of its creation.

NOTE ON ORTHOGRAPHY

Chinese names have been transliterated using Pinyin equivalents, with four main exceptions: two cities, Peking and Canton; and two people, Mao Tse-tung and Chou En-lai. These have been given in their older, more familiar, forms.

Foreword

by Andreas Whittam Smith

Newspaper reports, it is sometimes said, are the first rough drafts of history. It is a flattering phrase, suggesting more coherence than is often possible. In the case of the massacre around Tiananmen Square, and the events in Peking which led up to it, correspondents and cameramen recorded what they saw, analysed what they could, and, when necessary, risked their lives to do so. But it was impossible to comprehend this great story in the round. What was happening elsewhere in China? How did the government evaluate the situation? What did ordinary people think? These questions could not then be answered. From the flowering of China's democracy movement in the late spring days of April 1989 to the disaster on that June weekend, observers struggled to find explanations and make forecasts, conscious that they were dealing with something completely new.

The whole world watched as if transfixed. After the triumph of democracy in the Philippines and its failure in Burma, after Argentina's removal of army rule and Chile's loosening of a dictator's grip, after Solidarity's success in Poland and Charter 77's rebuffs in Czechoslovakia, after *perestroika* in the Soviet Union, could China be moving, politically, in a similar direction? There was the same naïvety, the same nobility. When confronting the army in the last dreadful moments before Tiananmen Square was cleared, the student leaders refused to arm themselves, saying: "We demonstrate in peace, and the most supreme principle of peace is to give up our lives."

Many made the supreme sacrifice, and thus elevated their defeat into an event of enormous resonance. Like the Hungarian uprising of 1956 and the Prague Spring of 1968, it has become one of those few, seemingly lost, causes which stay forever in the mind. "How could they?" we ask of both sides, as we reflect on the courage and the cruelty.

Wherever there is a yearning for freedom, the Chinese democracy movement of 1989 will be an inspiration, a lesson and a warning.

For precisely this reason, the Chinese government has laboured to persuade its people that events which Western observers and the residents of Peking know they saw, never really happened. Thugs had indulged in rumour-mongering and incitement. They had attacked the People's Liberation Army and had intended to create worse turmoil. To convey this impression, television film has been cut and edited. School-children are compelled to study texts which support it. The country's leaders have worked assiduously to propagate the Big Lie.

Among those who know the Big Lie for what it is are *The Independent*'s five reporters and two photographers who were in China during the fateful weeks. This book is written by two of them: the newspaper's Peking correspondent, Andrew Higgins, and its Asia editor, Michael Fathers. Both are brave men and fine reporters, never missing a deadline even when caught up in the fighting. Indeed, Mr Fathers was severely beaten up by the army, but filed his story of the incident on time.

This account is, in effect, a second and more complete draft of the origins, the successes and the apparent failure of the democracy movement. It draws on many reports unavailable to a single correspondent at the time, and upon subsequent interviews with participants. It uses the perspective which comes from standing back a few weeks from the tumultuous days. The reactions, fears, hopes and motives of the Chinese leadership have become much clearer.

After the reporters will come the historians. Until then, let this stand as the best answer available to those insistent questions — what really happened, and what does it all portend?

London, August 16th 1989

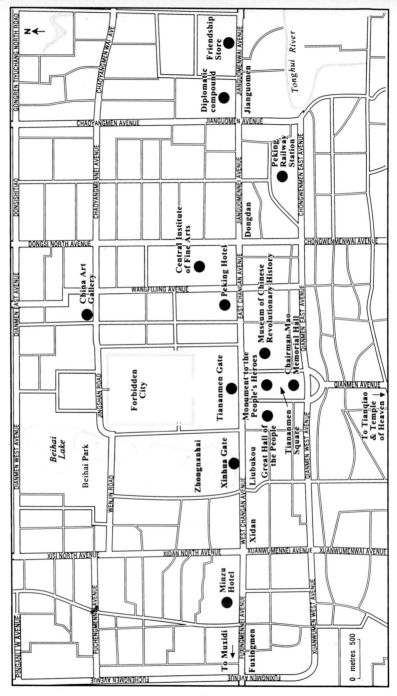

DRAMATIS PERSONAE

The Older Leaders:
Deng Xiaoping, 84, ruler of China
Yang Shangkun, 82, State President

The Standing Committee of the Politburo at April 15 1989:
Zhao Ziyang, 70, Communist Party general secretary
Li Peng, 61, prime minister
Qiao Shi, 65, vice-premier
Yao Yilin, 72, vice-premier
Hu Qili, 60

Peking Officials:
Li Ximing, 63, Communist Party secretary
Chen Xitong, 59, mayor

The Students:
Wang Dan, early 20s, Peking University
Wuerkaixi, 21, Peking Normal University
Chai Ling, 23, Peking Normal University

INTRODUCTION

"Anyone should be allowed to speak out, whoever he may be, as long as he is not a hostile element." With this maxim, in 1945, Mao Tse-tung defined the limits of democracy in Communist China.

During the extraordinary Peking Spring of 1989, hundreds of thousands of young Chinese thought they had broken free from that intellectual straitjacket, as they gathered to call for democracy, freedom of the press and an end to official corruption and nepotism. They had reckoned without the unchanging attitudes of Mao's successors. The economy could be freed, decreed Deng Xiaoping, China's ruler. But not the mind.

On October 1 1949, in Tiananmen Square, at the gates of the Forbidden City in the heart of Peking, Mao had announced the founding of the People's Republic of China. On June 3-4 1989, Deng and his octogenarian cronies unleashed a military assault on thousands of unarmed students in that same Square, to defend, as they imagined, that same Republic which they had fought alongside Mao to establish 40 years earlier.

The old men did not understand debate, only struggle. They divided their world into two armed camps: the Party, and the conspiracy against it. Where others saw innocents in their teens and twenties thronging Tiananmen Square, the model of peaceful idealism, Deng saw old enemies in new guises returning to pursue the unfinished anti-Socialist battles of decades past: the "class enemies", the "imperialists", and even, it would later be said, the remnants of the "Gang of Four", radical Maoists whose bid for power in the later stages of the Cultural Revolution had meant humiliation and banishment for Deng, President Yang Shangkun and almost all of their contemporaries in power.

Such memories haunted the old men. They saw no distinction between democracy and chaos, only between chaos and the strong leadership of the Communist Party. Deng remembered what "democracy" had been taken to mean during the Cultural Revolution, when mob rule had brought China to the verge of anarchy. "People thought that rousing the masses to headlong action was democracy, and that it would solve all problems. But it turned out that when the masses were aroused the result was civil war. We have learned our lesson from history." He also knew that democracy could mean the end of absolute Communist Party power — and that this was not politics, but treason. "The key point," he said after the students had been crushed, "is that they wanted to overthrow *our* State, and *our* Party."

The explosive events of April, May and June were the product of tensions which had been building up in China for more than a decade; tensions between economic reform and political stagnation. Individualism and responsibility were encouraged in the workplace, but denied in society. Western technology and expertise were imported wholesale, but Western values and aspirations were denounced. As Deng said in his speech to army generals after the Tiananmen assault, "The storm was inevitable".

The protests grew out of mourning for the death of Hu Yaobang, the deposed Communist Party leader, on April 15. On April 26, as mass rallies and boycotts paralysed Peking campuses, the Party declared that a "grave political struggle" was underway. But when it reached for its traditional tools of control — threats, harassment, strident newspaper editorials — it found them to be ineffective. The students were not being isolated and humiliated. Instead, they were gaining allies among the ordinary people, not only of Peking, but of cities throughout China. As the spectacle of defiance grew, so too did the conviction of hardliners within the Communist leadership that only an exemplary show of violence could restore the Party's unchallenged authority. In anger and desperation, they called upon the People's Liberation Army.

From the point at which Martial Law was declared on May 20, there could be no turning back for the group backed by Deng which had demanded it. They had characterized the student movement as turmoil, conspiracy, rebellion, and eventually "counter-revolution". They had shouted down their colleagues who counselled patience. They had warned that the Party could no longer afford to tolerate dissent, or accommodate debate. They had brought the People's Liberation Army into the suburbs of Peking, ready for battle. Their judgement, their credibility, was in question. If the turmoil did not exist, it would have to be created.

By any humane criteria, the assault of June 3-4 was futile, random, insane. The students had attacked nobody and damaged nothing. But those who ordered the attack were not aiming simply to disperse a demonstration. They were seeking to eradicate, through terror, the idea that *any* direct challenge could be mounted to their own authority. Their targets were not only those people still on the streets of Peking, but all who sympathized with them, both inside and outside the Party. Opposition had to be *seen* to be crushed.

"War is the highest form of struggle for resolving contradictions," wrote Mao Tse-tung. "War is the continuation of politics." War was what Peking got.

CHAPTER ONE

An untimely death

It began as it would end: with white paper flowers on the campus of Peking University. They put them up when people died.

China's democracy movement died shortly before midnight on the evening of Saturday June 3, when the People's Liberation Army first opened fire on the residents of Peking. Its birth could be identified with still greater precision: at 3.02 on the afternoon of Saturday April 15. It was then that Radio Peking announced the death of Hu Yaobang, the short and peppery Politburo member who had, until his disgrace two years previously, been general secretary of the Chinese Communist Party.

Within minutes of the announcement, students and teachers began to gather around notice boards near the main canteen of Peking University, about seven miles north of the city centre. Timidly at first, they stuck up messages of mourning. Then, across the campus, the paper flowers blossomed, twists of crumpled white tissue bunched together with wire and string to signify mourning. By evening they could be seen dangling from trees, strung from balconies and woven together to form funeral wreaths.

Even the first, unpremeditated tributes to Hu carried with them an edginess hinting at the confrontation ahead. "A true man has died," read one scrawled in black ink on old newspaper, "false men are still living." A second dealt more pointedly with the accident of fate which had allowed the far older Deng Xiaoping, China's ruler since 1978, to outlive his former protégé: "Xiaoping is still healthy at the age of 84. Yaobang, only 73 years old, has died first." The author's regret at this turn of events was clear, if unstated. Others were still blunter: "The wrong man has died ... Those who should die still live. Those who should live have died." Such messages would recur time and again in

4

the weeks ahead: the leadership, particularly Deng, had lost the confidence of the people.

Hu was a loyal — if, at the time of his death, aggrieved — servant of the revolution, and as much a man of the Communist Party system as those other leaders whom the Peking students were attacking in his name. The son of poor peasants, he received little, if any, formal education before running away from home to join the Communist army. He was one of the youngest survivors of the 1934-35 Long March, in the course of which he became a life-long friend of Deng Xiaoping. When Deng emerged as China's effective leader, and needed a safe pair of hands to run the Party organisation, it was Hu he chose to be general secretary. Hu was widely respected as the model of the loyal, honest official, who dared speak his mind. He was, in his own words, "not a man of iron ... but a man of passion, of flesh and blood".

Even Hu's death was down to earth: he suffered a massive heart attack while sitting on the lavatory in a Peking military hospital. Radio Peking, announcing his death six hours later, said simply: "He was given all possible medical attention but to no avail. To our great sorrow, he died at 07.53 on April 15 1989 at the age of 73."

Hu had, in fact, been ill for several months, and had suffered an earlier heart attack at New Year while visiting his home province of Hunan in southern China. But news of his condition was kept secret from the general public, partly because the health of Chinese leaders had always been a taboo subject, but perhaps also because more sensitive antennae within the leadership realized just how emotive his death might prove to be.

The grief that first Saturday at Peking University was tinged with excitement. Funerals of Chinese leaders offered the opportunity for protest as well as mourning — as had been the case, most notably, in 1976, when cancer claimed the moderate and much-loved Chou En-lai, who had served as Mao Tse-tung's prime minister for 27 years. Chou died in January. In the weeks which followed, with Mao himself on his deathbed, radical left-wingers within the Party tried to stifle public mourning. For several months they succeeded. But in April, during the Qing Ming Festival when Chinese traditionally honoured their dead, the dam burst. Tens of thousands poured into Tiananmen Square, laying wreaths and poems of mourning and speaking out in defiance of Mao's detested wife, Jiang Qing, and the other radicals. Police were ordered to clear the Square by force — a course of action which was later used by moderates within the Party to discredit the radicals, and served as a catalyst for the latter's downfall.

Like Chou, Hu could inspire genuine affection rather than the fawning flattery more usual within the Party. He was, despite his background, an especially attractive figure to China's academics and artists, for whom his fall from grace was a sad and cautionary tale. Having attempted, as Party boss, to pay something more than lip service to intellectual freedom, he was brought down by a seemingly immovable coalition of octogenarian veterans, supported by an only slightly younger band of hardline ideologues.

Hu was forced to resign in January 1987, six years after his appointment. He was blamed for a series of student demonstrations in Shanghai, Peking and other cities across the country which, though far smaller and more temperate than those which would be triggered by his death, gave his enemies the pretext they needed to turn Deng against him. Hu was, they held, too soft on "bourgeois liberalism" — Party code for anything which challenged the Stalinist political structures in place since the 1949 revolution. But another, far more trivial accusation which formed part of the official indictment against Hu gave a better indication of the real reasons for his fall: he had failed to pay his respects to his elders at Chinese New Year. He had, in other words, presumed himself to be something more than an obedient servant. He had attempted, as general secretary of the Communist Party, to wield the power which that office should possess. He had shown himself willing to challenge the veterans' vision of how China should be run, and, more importantly, their personal right to run it. By doing so, he sealed his fate.

Hu, though not a "liberal" in any Western sense of the word, was a modernizer. He enraged many veterans and embarrassed even his supporters with his sometimes clownish attempts to prove his commitment to reform. He was the first senior leader to wear a Western business suit instead of the traditional Mao jacket, though he often did so with long underwear sticking out from ill-fitting trousers. He even urged people to give up chopsticks and start eating with knives and forks so as to avoid contagious diseases. Had his innovations been limited to such buffoonery, he would probably have survived. But he went further. In 1984, he informed the world, through the columns of

People's Daily, that "Marx and Lenin can't solve our problems." Two days later, the paper issued a correction. Hu had meant to say "can't solve *all* our problems".

Hu thought that the modernisation of China meant something more than the acquisition of Western technology: he thought that the political system would have to change, too. In fact, he even seemed to believe that it *had* changed, telling one interviewer that China had "abolished the practice of putting emphasis on the role of one man's power". Worse still, he threatened the Old Guard on a personal level by attacking the privileges and corruption which bonded them and their offspring to power. He threatened to launch a "tiger hunt", an anti-corruption drive which would penetrate the upper reaches of the Party and military hierarchy. Finally, in the summer of 1986, he committed an unforgivable act of *lèse-majesté* by urging all veteran leaders, including Deng, to retire from office.

Less than six months later, it was Hu, not the veterans, who was out of a job. Even his supposed ally, Zhao Ziyang, the prime minister, had let him down, and been rewarded with a promotion to Hu's own former job. Dispirited and disgusted, he retired to his courtyard home at Number 25 Kuaijisi ("Accountant") Alley, a side-street near the Forbidden City, where he studied classical texts on political intrigue during the Ming and Ch'ing dynasties.

Though he remained a member of the Politburo*, he rarely took any active role in policy-making. On one issue, however, he continued to try to make his voice heard. This was education, a field which in China embraced more than textbooks and classrooms. Education was, not least, the means through which the Party established its authority and power among succeeding generations. "Inadequate development" of education, Deng said in March 1989, was the "greatest mistake made by China over the past ten years."

The Politburo was divided. Reformists worried about the years of anti-intellectualism, under-funding and general neglect which had left professors earning less than taxi drivers, and students living in squalor. They warned, correctly, that this was a recipe for social disaster. The

---

*   The executive arm of the Central Committee

very people most central to China's modernisation were being alienated. Something had to be done to reward them for their labours. Conservatives replied that the real crisis was not financial, but ideological. Schools had forgotten their main function — the inculcation of patriotism and socialist values. They should worry less about pampering freethinkers and more about forming the front line against the spread of "bourgeois liberalism". Without such defences, the conservatives warned — also correctly — the campuses would become breeding grounds for dissent and disappointment.

Hu sided with the reformists. Though purged for refusing to combat "bourgeois liberalism", he continued to argue that education should serve modernisation rather than abstract ideology. His determination to express this view led him, despite his ill-health, to attend an important Politburo meeting on April 8, to discuss a policy document on education which had been in preparation for a period of months, but over which wide differences of opinion still remained. About 40 minutes after the meeting began, while Li Tieying, the Politburo member responsible for education, was talking, Hu collapsed. What triggered the sudden attack has not, and may never be, revealed. The most detailed account of the incident came from the official China News Service which, in a report issued a week later, immediately after his death, said only that "A Politburo member immediately put some highly efficacious heart disease medicine into his mouth and Hu Yaobang was rushed to Peking hospital for emergency treatment".

The April 8 incident evidently left other Politburo members worried about the rumours which would inevitably follow. Li Peng, the prime minister, took pains several days later to deny any direct link between the debate and the seizure. Before leaving for Japan on April 12, he said he wanted to "point out the fact that (Hu's illness) had nothing directly to do with the Politburo meeting" — an extraordinary disclaimer, and one which hinted at the extreme tensions which had been building up within the leadership.

THE MAINSPRING of those tensions was China's programme of economic reforms, the portfolio name for attempts to reconcile Marx with the modern world. Zhao Ziyang and his followers wanted to press ahead towards more of a market-based economy, implicitly accepting whatever pressure for analogous social and political developments this might provoke. Conservatives, led by a clutch of elderly and semi-retired leaders of whom Li Peng* was a protégé, were suspicious of any sweeping innovations, for fear that they might loosen the Party's absolute grip on power and undermine the stability of the State. Each side blamed the other for the increasingly erratic performance of the economy, and for the Party's recent inability to meet the rising expectations which the early years of Deng's decade-long rule had encouraged among the people.

The main policy battles of 1988 had been fought over prices: whether they should be set by the State or by market forces. Reformists said market forces would allocate resources more efficiently than the State; conservatives that the State was wiser than the markets. In practice, the arguments over price reform would be resolved in the same way as most other arguments over most other subjects in China: by Deng Xiaoping.

It did not matter that Deng, then 83, had formally retired from the Party's Central Committee in 1987. His power endured, and he alone gave the stamp of final authority to major policy decisions. In the spring of 1988, he threw his weight behind a radical shift to market-determined prices. Short-term pain, he said, was better than long-term agony. Zhao, moving into his second year as Party general secretary, made the policy public. "We are ready," he said, "despite the risk."

By autumn, it was clear that the risks were rather greater than Zhao or Deng had expected. Inflation was running at its highest level since the 1949 revolution. Panic-buying swept major Chinese cities. Shoddy goods which had lain collecting dust for years were being snapped up by consumers desperate for any hedge against rising prices. As faith in the currency was eroded, there were bank runs in Shanghai and other cities. Urban residents, the worst sufferers, were increasingly ready to show their anger in sporadic acts of violence. Peasants, many of whom had been paid for their last crops with IOUs written on white slips, were also restive. For the old Communists who remembered the hyper-inflation which undermined Chiang Kai-shek's Nationalist regime, these were sobering days. Authority, it seemed, had collapsed, at least where

---

*　　The adoptive son of Chou En-lai

9

the economy was concerned. Could a collapse of political authority be far behind?

The leadership did not cling long to its course. By the end of 1988, after a divisive meeting at Beidaihe, its summer retreat, it restored many of the controls which it had previously lifted. Economic reform lurched into abeyance. Little more was heard about "braving the storm" or "storming the pass" or any other of Deng's earlier swashbuckling slogans. In their place came a new, more stolid catchphrase: "Rectification of the economic order and improvement of the economic environment." Discretion had become the better part of valour.

The significance of this about-turn went far beyond the direct economic consequences. By creating new conventional wisdoms as to which policies had succeeded and which had failed, it created a new balance of prestige within the leadership. The champions of reform, led by Zhao, suffered a severe setback, while the fortunes of the conservative faction, headed within the Politburo by Li Peng and Yao Yilin, were advanced. Crucially, events also restored credibility to the Party elders whom Deng had previously tried to push aside and whose advice he had tried to ignore — veteran planners such as Chen Yun, now sidelined to the Party's Central Advisory Commission, and Li Xiannian, who had been Mao Tse-tung's finance minister before the Cultural Revolution and Deng's state president after it. Both had been warning for years of the perils of relaxing controls too far, too fast. Deng was now forced to admit, privately, that they had been right.

Because Deng was all but untouchable, it was Zhao who took the blame. When Li Peng spoke to the National People's Congress, China's parliament, in March 1989, it was with a fresh and pointed confidence. He dwelt on what he called "shortcomings and mistakes in our guidance", remarks outwardly cast as a self-criticism on behalf of the entire leadership. But all those on the podium knew that Li's real target was the man sitting just behind the lectern from which he spoke: Zhao Ziyang. The one man who might have shielded Zhao, Deng Xiaoping, was absent — because, he later said gnomically, he had "wanted to live longer".

Li proposed a new course: a renewed emphasis on ideology as the organizing principle of Chinese society. People should, he said, "oppose putting money above all else" — an oblique but fundamental shift from the motto of the previous decade, "To get rich is glorious". It was as if Li realized that neither he, Zhao nor anyone else was going to sort out China's economic mess in the near future, and that the Party would do well to stop measuring its own worth in terms of rising living standards. Political stability could not be allowed to rest on material aspirations which the Party might not be able to realize. Instead, it must be seen to rest upon the authority of the Party itself. Such authority would, in turn, have to be unchallenged.

Li's argument found ready listeners among those who worried that the Party was losing its grip. Shortly before the Congress session, Tibet had exploded into its most serious violence since the abortive uprising 30 years before. Though the "enemy" was for the most part unarmed monks, the leadership was deeply shaken, and determined that the correct solution was a terrifying show of force. It declared Martial Law, and sent in convoys of armoured vehicles carrying thousands of troops. Local aspirations to self-determination were denounced. "The Lhasa riots have their own particular background," *People's Daily* said in a front-page editorial on March 14, "but they show how we must value a stable environment ... Haste and impatience for progress on the question of democracy will only increase the sources of instability." Critical precedents had been set.

CHAPTER TWO

Power and the past

TWO thousand miles separated Peking from the most distant of its frontiers, across the sprawling mass of a China united only by the ubiquity of its Communist Party apparatus. For political power to be transmitted to such distant fringes, it needed to be generated in immense quantities at the centre. Under Deng, as under Mao and under the emperors before them, the primary purpose of China's capital city had been to manifest the authority of the ruler who dwelt within it.

For centuries, the epicentre of that authority had been the vast, sterile expanse of Tiananmen Square, the "Gate of Heavenly Peace", around which ranged China's historic centres of power. Its name derived from that of the gate to the Imperial Palace, the "Forbidden City", which lay to the north. Ming and Ch'ing dynasty emperors ruled there for five centuries until 1911, believing their domain to be the centre of the world, and themselves to partake of divinity. They rarely ventured outside the 20-foot-high palace walls, but had their proclamations declaimed from Tiananmen Gate to the vulgar world outside.

With perhaps too nice a sense of irony, Mao Tse-tung chose Tiananmen Gate as the spot from which, on October 1 1949, he read an edict of his own, proclaiming the foundation of the People's Republic of China. To prepare for the tenth anniversary of that occasion in 1959, he extended the Square from 27 to 100 acres, razed the houses and lanes on its southern edge, and ordered the erection of monumental buildings around its margin. The biggest of these, the Great Hall of the People, on the western side of Tiananmen Square, would be the ceremonial seat of his own government.

In 1989, two rival traditions of Chinese politics would collide in Tiananmen Square. One was that of Communist Party orthodoxy, its eyes fixed on the 40th anniversary of Mao's greatest achievement. The other was that of China's intellectuals, their eyes cast back 30 years further still, to an event which, though it lasted a single afternoon, changed attitudes which had endured among them for centuries.

On May 4 1919, three thousand students marched from Peking University to Tiananmen Square to voice their outrage at China's humiliation in the Versailles Peace Conference. There, ignoring China's pleas, the victors of the First World War had ruled that Tokyo, not Peking, should recover Germany's colonial claims along the Chinese coast. Though the demonstration was triggered by a spasm of patriotic indignation, it quickly laid bare other, more complex emotions.

The students declared that China's sufferings were the product of its own weakness, of the corruption of its political system under warlord rule. Animated by the dream of a "new China", the May Fourth Movement marked the point at which they began systematically to question the values into which they were being educated, and to look outward for ideas and experiences which could not adequately be judged by the hermeneutic standards of Chinese courtly culture. They called for democracy and science. They would no longer be passive servants of the emperor or warlord, but catalysts for political change. By these leaps of the imagination, they ushered in a period of intellectual ferment unequalled, some said, since the age of Confucius more than 2,000 years before.

For the Chinese intellectuals of 1989, the 70th anniversary of May 4 meant a chance to revive the unfulfilled hopes launched by that first, rag-tag procession to Tiananmen. While the Communist Party was fretting about its failing economic policies, China's students, teachers, writers and other intellectuals, who had suffered often enough under Mao, were discovering new courage and vigour. They were calling for democracy, for freedom, for an end to China's "feudal" tradition of rule by man and for the introduction of rule by law.

The Communist Party, which liked to think of the May Fourth Movement as one milestone along its own triumphant road, faced a dilemma. Many of its historic leaders, including Chou En-lai, had been active in the movement. The intellectual renaissance which it triggered had given Mao Tse-tung and others their first introduction to Marxism, and had clearly been central to the founding of the Party two years later. But, at the same time, the movement encouraged demands which were as much a threat to the orthodoxy of communism in 1989 as they had been to that of Confucianism 70 years before.

The Party tried to contain the implied threat by ensuring that the anniversary was celebrated on its own terms. It unleashed a flood-tide of "official" commemorative seminars, films, books and articles, all of which echoed a single theme: the celebration of May 4 as a "patriotic" event which paved the way for communism. Notions of democracy, and other political ideas so important to the original movement, would be ignored.

But the Party could only dampen the resonances of May 4, not eliminate them. The momentum of dissent had been building up in university campuses, research centres and newspapers across China for many months. As it happened, the trigger which released these passions came not on May 4, but a fortnight earlier, with the death of Hu Yaobang. But as Chen Xitong, the mayor of Peking, later remarked, the death of Hu was like "a match thrown into a barrel of waiting gunpowder".

THE PARTY, worried by the precedent of Chou En-lai's mourners, moved quickly on April 15 to claim Hu's memory as their own. Within four hours of the announcement of death, Radio Peking broadcast an official obituary issued by the Central Committee. This made no mention of Hu's ejection from the office of general secretary two years earlier, nor of his alleged mistakes. Instead, it praised him as "a loyal fighter for communism, a great proletarian revolutionary, a great statesman" and said his life had "conferred lasting benefits on the Party and the people". A glowing tribute, from the very men who had conspired against him.

Few were convinced. Soon after the first posters appeared at Peking University, the mourning had spread to many other Peking campuses. Ordinary people were stirred, if not as grief-stricken as they had been for Chou. Newspaper kiosks reported that, for the first time in years, they had sold out of the *People's Daily*.

Each new wall poster confirmed that a political movement, albeit without organisation, was taking shape. "This is not just for Hu Yaobang," the scientist and dissident, Fang Lizhi, told reporters at his flat in Peking that first weekend. "This is a chance for students to let the government know they are unhappy with the present situation." The significance of Hu's death was expanding to embrace everything that needed to be changed in the Communist Party system. The author of one wall poem apostrophized Hu in these terms: "You died of a heart attack, but in your heart was China — China is sick."

The students did not yet have the courage to assail Hu's enemies directly. Instead, by demanding his full rehabilitation, they sought to manoeuvre the surviving leaders into admitting that they had made a mistake in sacking him. One poster, signed by 18 people at Peking University, called for a "public clarification" of the forced resignation and demanded that Hu's remains be placed alongside Mao's embalmed corpse in the Mausoleum on Tiananmen Square. Such an honour had been given to none other among the Great Helmsman's survivors.

That first weekend, students began to stake their claim to Tiananmen Square. First came more clusters of small white flowers and pieces of black cloth, tied to the iron chain barriers around the Monument to the People's Heroes, the 60-foot-high terraced obelisk erected at the centre of the Square in memory of those who died for Mao's revolution. Then, on Monday April 17, the first wreaths appeared at the base of the column, each with a white sash bearing the name of the mourners — the North China Transport University, the Agriculture Engineering University and other institutions. They bespoke a cross-section of Peking colleges extending far beyond the traditional centres of student militancy. More revealing still was the presence of a wreath from what should have been a bastion of obedience, the Communist Party History Faculty of the People's University, which specialized in the training of future cadres and government officials. One of its students was Mao Xinyu, the 19-year-old grandson of Mao Tse-tung.

The first procession to the Square began that same Monday afternoon. It was also the first illegal act. For though the Chinese constitution in theory guaranteed the right to stage marches and demonstrations, that right — like other such freedoms — had been emasculated in practice by successive local and national regulations. After the 1986-87 student protests, Peking municipal authorities had declared all marches to be illegal without prior approval from the police — a privilege granted only to supporters of the government.

Could the police crack down on what purported to be no more than an outpouring of respect for a man whom the Party had proclaimed a hero? The students thought not. "They can't stop us from commemorating a former Communist Party head, no matter how uncomfortable it makes them feel," said one. The calculation proved correct. Police looked on as the first marchers passed by, intervening only to free snarled traffic. They also kept themselves busy, taking photographs. Peking's public security apparatus was sometimes passive, but it was never idle.

The first march was small: a few hundred young students and teachers from the China University of Politics and Law. They marched 10 miles from the western suburbs carrying a wreath, a red cotton banner with the characters of the law faculty painted in gold on it and a cardboard placard bearing four black characters: "Yaobang lives for ever." Accompanied by blasts of a funeral dirge from a portable cassette player, they sang the Socialist anthem, the *Internationale*, in Chinese. They marched once around Tiananmen Square, moved on to its sacred stones at four in the afternoon, and placed their wreath on the Heroes' Monument. As they crossed the Square, they raised their fists and chanted: "Long Live Hu Yaobang. Long live democracy. Long live freedom. Down with corruption. Down with bureaucracy." The movement had found its slogans.

In the weeks that followed, Hu Yaobang would move down the agenda. Otherwise, the chants would stay much the same, but growing louder each day. Their very monotony reflected a circumstance which was one of the students' main handicaps, and at the same time one of their principal strengths. Very few of them could explain what the slogans actually meant. They articulated neither a thought-out political theory nor any detailed blueprint for change. But the very vagueness of the demands meant that they could accommodate every popular grievance. The students, and later the ordinary people who joined them, were moved by a general sense of outrage against China's ossified political system, a system that had perhaps relaxed its grip since the death of Mao, but was still firmly based on the unchallenged authority of the Party and its autocratic ways.

CHAPTER THREE

Against the Party

The main obstacle to political change in China was Deng Xiaoping. Though he had godfathered the reform of the economy, he had ruled out any parallel reform of the political structure. "We cannot do without dictatorship," he said during the earlier, milder round of student disturbances in the winter of 1986-87. "We must not only affirm the need for it, but exercise it when necessary."

What Deng could not, or would not, recognize was that the drive to reform and modernize China's economy had inevitably set expectations in train, at least among the intellectual and professional classes, that politics and society would be reformed in their turn, as surely as night followed day. Already, the economic imperative had created a new respect for the ideas of academics and graduates, particularly those who had studied overseas. Contacts with foreigners were commonplace. Foreign trade and investment was a virtue and a necessity. Information was flowing freely into and out of China. These factors were changing the way in which educated and urban Chinese thought about China, and they were not being harnessed, in the way Deng wanted, to economic ends alone.

The intellectuals, whom Mao had condemned as China's "ninth stinking category", had not forgotten their past traumas. Deng himself had helped manage the notorious "Anti-Rightist" campaign against them in 1957, when tens of thousands were purged or imprisoned. But, like their predecessors on May 4 1919, they were beginning to believe that history was on their side. For the first time in decades, writers, artists and academics were meeting to debate China's future without fear of arrest or interference. Newspapers, particularly the Shanghai-based *World Economic Herald*, were exploring long-taboo subjects. Avant-garde art, once a criminal offence, won official acceptance with a large exhibition in China's most prestigious national gallery. With not a picture of toiling workers or peasants in sight, the show featured inflated condoms and giant plastic breasts. It proved satisfyingly shocking, and was even closed down briefly after a young woman opened fire on her own work in the name of creativity. Everything seemed possible, even permissible.

The cleverest of China's freethinkers was probably Fang Lizhi, whose lecture-room arguments for democracy helped inspire the 1986-87 wave of student protests, after which he lost his job as vice-president of the University of Science and Technology at Hefei. An internationally-renowned astrophysicist, he lived in Peking with his wife, Li Shuxian, a lecturer at Peking University. Fang shared the general optimism that intellectuals were now too important, even too strong, for the Party to crush. "We are far more independent than before," he said in February at the launch of a private book imprint called *New Enlightenment*. "We have been cheated before and we won't be cheated again."

Though the government would cast Fang as the main villain behind the "counter-revolutionary rebellion" of 1989, he played no direct role in the protests once they had begun. He had, however, taken one modest — and, at the time, seemingly harmless — step in early January, which proved to be of immense importance. He wrote a letter to Deng Xiaoping, calling for the release of political prisoners including Wei Jingsheng. Wei had been a leading activist in the "Democracy Wall" free speech movement ten years earlier. Now, he was serving a 15-year prison sentence for "counter-revolutionary crimes". His release, wrote Fang, would be "a humanitarian gesture and would have a beneficial effect on our social morality".

The letter went unanswered, at least by the authorities. But it was copied and distributed around the country by sympathizers. It provoked an extraordinary response. By February, at least four petitions had begun to circulate supporting Fang's proposal, signed by some of the best-known names in China's artistic and academic circles. These ranged from young poets to the prominent Marxist theoretician, Su Shaozhi, and the 89-year-old writer, Xie Bingxin, a Party loyalist. Not since the May Fourth Movement had such disparate intellectuals found a common cause.

At the end of March, after weeks of official silence, the petitioners received a formal answer. The National People's Congress found that there was "no need now" to free Wei, or any other prisoner. Informally, Fang had already learned which way the wind was blowing when he set out on February 26 to attend a banquet hosted by the visiting United States President, George Bush, at the Great Wall Sheraton Hotel in Peking. Other guests at the Texas-style barbecue were Li Peng, the prime minister, and Yang Shangkun, the state president. As the car carrying Fang, his wife and an American academic, Perry Link, drew near the Sheraton, police came out of the shadows to bar its way. Fang, they said, was "not on the guest list". He might indeed have received an invitation from the American Embassy, but others had decided otherwise. The message was clear: Chinese leaders would never sit down in the same room with those who challenged them.

AS THE first procession of wreath-bearing students reached Tiananmen Square on the afternoon of Monday April 17, Zhao Ziyang and other members of the Politburo were meeting inside the Great Hall of the People. The topic on the agenda was, appropriately, education — the same issue which had triggered Hu's first heart attack nine days earlier. The leadership was still deadlocked over the final form of its policy document. Searching for a consensus, Zhao had summoned the leaders of China's eight "democratic" parties, decorative but impotent vestiges of the political movements active before 1949, for a discussion.

Zhao gave the meeting his own version of what Deng had meant when, a month earlier, he spoke of education as "our biggest mistake". Deng, he said, had intended to embrace "school education and ideological and political work". But by placing political education at the end of the list, Zhao was daring to reinterpret Deng in conformity with his own, more liberal views. Deng later set the record straight, in a speech to army commanders. "What I meant was political education," he said. "And this doesn't apply to schools and students alone, but to the masses as a whole."

If Deng's view of political education was indoctrination, Peking students had other ideas. Twelve hours after the first march on Tiananmen, before dawn on the morning of Tuesday April 18, a second and more impressive crowd paraded past Zhongnanhai, the high-walled compound beside the Forbidden City within which China's leaders kept their grace-and-favour houses. More than 2,000 strong, its members had marched or cycled the seven miles from Peking University in darkness. Students from Peking Normal University had tried to join them but had been locked inside their campus. The marchers carried a 20 foot-long white banner emblazoned with the words "Soul of China", a decorous tribute to Hu.

When they had draped the banner around the Monument to the People's Heroes, their caution evaporated. A student dressed in mourning clothes —- white trousers and matching bandanna — clambered on to the pediment of the Monument to shout three demands: the rehabilitation of Hu, an official apology for unspecified policy mistakes and the dismissal of unnamed government leaders. It was a bizarre, almost surreal scene enacted out beneath the impassive gaze of Mao Tse-tung's portrait looking down from Tiananmen Gate. The students, no more than a dot in the vast expanse of Tiananmen, had presumed openly to challenge the infallibility of their leaders. Had they ended their protest at that point and gone back to their campus, the leadership could perhaps have forgiven them. The demand for a change of government was just too absurd.

They did not retreat. Many stayed on the Square to engage in a political debate. From their exchanges emerged a less outrageous, and, therefore, more threatening, stand. They formulated a series of specific grievances which the Party would find difficult wholly to ignore and which would form the basis of the following weeks' protests. Sitting together in a circle near the centre of the Square, as the sun rose through the early morning mist, they read out suggestions. Calls for press freedom were cheered. "Open the bank accounts of the leaders." Cheers again. "And their sons and daughters." Even more cheering. "And their mistresses." Giggles. A demand to control inflation was booed down ("too general"), as was a demand from one bemused peasant, at sea among bespectacled intellectuals, for an end to the free market economy and an increase in rice rations.

By mid-morning, the crowd had thinned to one or two hundred. But by now, they had drawn up a list of demands in the form of a petition, a far cry from the previous day's lone student shouting from the Monument. For centuries in China, the petitioning of the emperor had been a permissible channel for seeking redress, a legitimate expression of discontent. China's Communist rulers had respected the petitioner's right, in name at least. But they could rarely, if ever, have been asked to acknowledge demands comparable to those now making up the students' list. There were seven in all: clear the name of Hu Yaobang; repudiate past campaigns against "bourgeois liberalisation" and "spiritual pollution"; publish the income and assets of leaders and their relatives; allow free speech and a free press; increase funding for education; raise the salaries of teachers and other intellectuals; and abolish restrictions on street marches, including the effective ban on press reporting of such events.

Moving to the entrance of the Great Hall, the students vowed to stay until an official from the National People's Congress, which had its seat there, came out to meet them. A minor functionary finally did so, but rejected the petition and told them to go home. Though this dismissive attitude set the pattern for future official responses to student requests, the students had now set precedents of their own. They had held their first sit-in, and in doing so had identified the real weapons in their armoury: patience, determination, self-discipline, high spirits and sheer bloody-mindedness. "We can wait for days for an answer if we have to," said one student squatting outside the Great Hall. "China has waited for years for democracy."

They did not, in the event, have to wait years, or even days. At eight o'clock that same evening, three members of the National People's Congress emerged to receive the petition. Its contents, they promised, would be passed on to "superior government departments". But the students wanted more. They had the advantage, they believed, and were determined to press it for all it was worth. They would stay.

THE PERSON behind this fateful decision was a scrawny, myopic history student from Peking University. Seven weeks later, his name, Wang Dan, would head the list of China's most wanted "counter-revolutionary ringleaders" — a cruel tribute to his critical role that first Tuesday. In the pre-dawn hours, when spirits had flagged and students were beginning to drift away, Wang Dan had proved himself a leader of unusual nerve and determination. Timid, uncharismatic, almost girlish in appearance, soft-spoken with a husky Peking accent, he was one of the few students with any experience in political organisation.

For the previous year, Wang had arranged seminars, called "Democracy Salons", on the lawns of Peking University. The discussions rarely attracted more than a few dozen people. Most of his classmates were too apathetic, or fearful of bad job assignments after graduation. At Tiananmen, he became the student movement's first real tactician. When the authorities wanted to argue that the protests were a "planned, organized and premeditated political turmoil, designed to negate the Communist Party leadership and the socialist system", Wang — who had come into contact with Fang Lizhi and Li Shuxian through his "salons" — would form a key link in their imagined conspiracy.

The decision to stay put in Tiananmen Square changed everything. Students across Peking now had not only a legitimate cause for demonstration, the death of Hu Yaobang, they also had among themselves the beginnings of a strategy. "We have woken up," read one banner brought to the Square that day. Thousands had started flowing into Tiananmen to lay wreaths, chant slogans, sing the *Internationale* and offer support to their colleagues before the Great Hall. The reverberations were felt in cities across China. A thousand students took to the streets in Shanghai, again ostensibly to mourn Hu, but with more general discontent barely submerged. In the port city of Tianjin, students at Nankai University issued an open letter in support of their Peking colleagues and called for united action. Recalling the ideals of the May Fourth Movement, they warned that "jackals and wolves now hold sway. There is no time to wait. Now is the time to act."

On Tuesday night, the protests in Peking grew more pointed and aggressive. Shortly before eleven o'clock, a young crowd of several thousand, most of them students, left Tiananmen Square and headed for Zhongnanhai. A shoving match broke out with startled guards protecting the entrance to this inner sanctum. From the students then came a cry for which they would later pay dearly: "Li Peng come out, Li Peng come out." Throwing off the camouflage of mourning and turning their attentions from the dead to the living, they instinctively targeted the prime minister, a short-tempered machine politician of authoritarian views, as the embodiment of the nepotistic oligarchy which they despised.

Li Peng, of course, did not come out. Enraged, several hundred students, some bearing funeral wreaths, tried to force their way beyond the red-lacquered gateway and past the screen which had been placed there, in conformity with traditional belief, to block out evil spirits. The screen was illuminated with calligraphy in Mao's hand, of his favourite motto: "Serve the People." Guards, locking arms to form a human wall, stood their ground and held back the crowd. As the older leaders must have reflected, such scenes of youthful chaos and disrespect had not been seen in Peking since the Cultural Revolution ended, 13 years before.

Until now, the leadership had made an outward show of tolerance. After the incident at Zhongnanhai, official reaction was swift. At 4.20 on Wednesday morning, after hours of standoff, police loudspeakers around the compound came to life. They broadcast a decree, the first of many, from the Peking Municipal Government. Minutes later, a thousand or more police officers arrived to clear the area. Mourning for Hu Yaobang was understandable, the loudspeakers announced, but things had gone too far. A "small number of people" had begun "spreading rumours, poisoning people's minds, putting up big character posters attacking and insulting Party and government leaders".

On Wednesday, the crowds grew bigger still. Some 30,000 or more thronged Tiananmen Square. Dozens more wreaths arrived to clutter the Monument to the People's Heroes, some from colleges, others from within the Party itself. By the end of the day, the obelisk was piled high with tributes to Hu. One wreath came from the *People's Daily*, the mouthpiece of the Party Central Committee, another from the Communist Youth League, where Hu had spent much of his career. Students from the Central Institute of Fine Art paraded into the Square carrying a giant black and white portrait of Hu, which, in a provocative affront to the Party's Old Guard, they hoisted atop the granite pedestal of the Heroes' Monument, from where it stared out unflinchingly towards the portrait of Mao on Tiananmen Gate. It was as if Peking suddenly had two rival sources of authority, the two patrons of different visions of communism staring each other down across the Square.

Next to Hu's portrait hung a large placard, reading simply: "Overthrow dictatorship". Students voiced the same theme in speeches from the Monument. "The old views and system can't satisfy the people anymore," one speaker yelled to the crowd. "Hu Yaobang didn't have a foreign bank account," said another. Others criticized the surviving leaders, as well as the system which they had created. "Let Tzu Hsi retire," shouted one student in an oblique reference to Deng Xiaoping, who — like the Empress Dowager Tzu Hsi at the end of the 19th century — continued to rule long after promising to retire.

Though the crowds grew still bigger and more boisterous in their demands, police made no effort to intervene. Emboldened by this apparent immunity, that Wednesday night the students staged a second, larger protest outside Zhongnanhai. Again they called for Li Peng to come out, and again no one came. Curious onlookers swelled their number to about 10,000. Each time they rushed the heavily-guarded entrance, the guards managed to hold them back. The crowd roared abuse: "Running dogs go away ... Do not beat the people ... Down with dictatorship." Hundreds of police arrived to reinforce security. But, at the very moment when conflict seemed inevitable, cooler heads prevailed. Many of the casual participants had already begun to drift away when the students withdrew from the Xinhua (New China) Gate, the main entrance to the compound, to begin a sit-in outside on Changan Avenue.[*]

Just as the first sit-in outside the Great Hall of the People had thrust Wang Dan into the forefront of the student movement, this second display of passive resistance produced another key student leader. He was a swaggering young man called Uerkesh Daolet, a 21-year-old education student from Chinese Turkestan in his second year at Peking Normal University, better-known to his friends and teachers by his Sinicised name of Wuerkaixi. "I knew that we needed an organizer who wasn't afraid to die," he would say later with characteristic bravado, commenting on his first foray into street politics that night. Two months later, he would figure second behind Wang Dan on the list of the 21 most-wanted student leaders, "the ringleaders and backbone elements" of a counter-revolution.

If Wang Dan was the calm, almost scholarly tactician, Wuerkaixi represented the other extreme. Against the former's black cotton shoes and drab baggy clothes, Wuerkaixi sported boots and a washed denim jacket. As much a showman as a committed activist, he relished attention. A good and often amusing speaker, he had an ability unique among the students to cajole and charm crowds. Most important of all,

---

[*]   Changan, the "Avenue of Eternal Peace", is Peking's main east-west artery. It is called
       loosely by this name throughout most of its western length, though its official
       designation changes several times outside the city centre.

he had boundless faith in his own abilities. Asked several weeks later what had made the student movement of 1989 so much bigger than any that preceded it, he replied simply: *"Wo"* — "Me".

Outside Zhongnanhai in the early hours of Thursday morning, such confidence was just what the students needed. Several had tried in vain to impose some discipline on the swirling mass. But, as Wuerkaixi later said: "They had no real ability. The situation needed someone like me ... I was extremely angry at the police, so I finally decided to stand up." Unmoved by the presence of hundreds of paramilitary officers, he shouted over the crowd for quiet and calm. His classmates from Peking Normal University were the first to obey. Other students followed. Before long, he had more than a thousand people sitting on the tarmac, listening intently as he led a freewheeling discussion, half theatre and half serious political debate.

Some students stood up to make speeches. Others, worried about how long the mood of euphoria could last, made comments or criticisms in writing. Scribbled on slips of paper, they would be handed to a bolder colleague and read to the crowd. "It was beautiful," Wuerkaixi commented later. "All they needed was a bit of organisation." Even the police seemed impressed. They stopped their advance, and some managed a smile. One slip of paper read to the crowd said: "As a representative of police fighters with a conscience, I support you." It was impossible to be sure whether or not the note was genuine. But whatever its true authorship, it hinted at the leadership's worst nightmare: that peaceful persuasion might begin to erode the very foundation of its power.

Shortly before four o'clock in the morning, police vans equipped with loudspeakers began to broadcast a new order from the Peking authorities. A woman's voice told the students to go home, echoing the previous day's warning that they should be on guard against a "small number of people" bent on stirring up trouble. The tone grew harsher. The voice said that protesters had not only blocked traffic and defied police, but had also committed the far graver crime of "chanting reactionary slogans calling for the overthrow of the Communist Party of China". It was the first time that the term "reactionary" had been attached to aspects of the protest movement, a term of condemnation second only to "counter-revolutionary" in the official lexicon.

Loudspeakers broadcast the announcement repeatedly. Intimidated, some students collected their bicycles and peddled away. Most stayed put. But any illusions which they might have had about winning over the security forces ended shortly before dawn when hundreds of police swarmed out of vehicles and side-streets nearby. The students' nerve broke; the sit-in disintegrated into panic. The few who refused to move were beaten and hit with leather belts. Others were hit as they ran away.

Though the violence was real enough, its scale was rapidly exaggerated by the students, who claimed their first "martyrs". As bedraggled participants of the sit-in returned to their colleges in driving rain on Thursday morning, new wall posters appeared on campuses calling for revenge. "The blood of our classmates will not be shed in vain," read one. "Since the time of the first emperor 2,000 years ago, China has been living under a dictatorship. It is time for this to end."

ANGER at the Zhongnanhai clash was the common factor needed to galvanize the disparate groups of protesting students into a single movement, with Peking University in the vanguard. When the smaller student protests had erupted in the winter of 1986, Shanghai, Hefei and other provincial cities had taken the lead. In the first week after Hu Yaobang's death, the Peking students saw themselves as renewing a glorious, long-dormant tradition, re-asserting their own place at the centre of Chinese political thought. They formed the first independent student organisation to emerge from those initial days of unrest, the cumbersomely-named Peking University Students' Solidarity Preparatory Committee, breaking free of the tightly-controlled official student unions which were little more than youth chapters of the Communist Party, their membership vetted and their activities closely supervised by the campus Party secretary. Some of its members quickly rose to prominence — or, as the government would have it, notoriety. They included Wang Dan, Xiong Yan, a law student, Yang Tao, a history student, and Feng Congde, the husband of Chai Ling, the *Passionara* of the student movement. Yang was 19, the others in their twenties.

The first action of the nine-member Preparatory Committee was to write a manifesto and plaster it over the notice-boards of Peking University in the form of a "big character poster". Called an "Open Letter to Peking Colleges", it was a turgid document written in the style of a Communist Party circular. Nonetheless, it provided the blueprint for the future student and for its tactics over the coming weeks. It called on students to unite under its "collective leadership", and enumerated the tactical weapons — sit-ins, protest marches, classroom strikes and hunger strikes — which would all be used to devastating effect in the coming weeks.

Though prepared by a committee composed mainly of teenagers, the poster bore the marks of more experienced, older students. Unlike their younger colleagues, they had bitter memories of previous attempts to mobilize on Chinese campuses. One such was Liu Gang, a 28-year-old former graduate student in physics at Peking University. Like others active behind the scenes in the spring of 1989, he had taken part in the 1986-87 protests, and had seen how the movement crumbled as soon as the authorities began to flex their muscles. The experience of men like Liu would prove indispensable. They knew the tactics of the Party; more importantly, knew how to copy them. For a time, it seemed as though they could even confound them.

The Preparatory Committee's promise of "collective leadership" was an attempt at binding together a movement plagued from the outset by internal divisions, reflecting the spontaneity of its creation and the lack of a clear focus other than discontent with the government. Personal rivalries and suspicion of infiltration were rife. Wuerkaixi acknowledged that it "could not completely follow democratic principles," but had to be lead by those with the courage to lead.

A painful example of the early disarray came with a rally on April 24 which drew 3,000 students to an open-air sports stadium at Peking University. It began on a triumphal note. Wang Dan, speaking from a score-keeper's box on the side of the stadium, told the students they were involved in the "greatest movement since May Fourth". Cheers rang out. "We are at an historical turning point. The leaders have seen what the power of the people is." Moments later, another speaker took the floor to denounce a colleague as an informer. Scuffles broke out over the microphone and accusations of treachery multiplied. The crowd drifted away in disgust, amid mutterings that the students were "worse than the Communist Party". But they were learning.

CHAPTER FOUR

Rites of Passage

The Party had fixed Hu's funeral for Saturday April 22, in the Great Hall of the People. Everything about the ceremony had been carefully planned to keep out interlopers. There was to be no public viewing of the body, no foreign delegations, and carefully-vetted guests. To avoid disturbances, the police announced that they would seal off Tiananmen Square and the surrounding streets from eight in the morning until mid-day.

On Friday night, Tiananmen was in ferment. Crowds of people, few of them students, swirled backwards and forwards looking for action, for some excitement to break the monotony of a balmy Peking evening. Some were clearly hoping for a repeat of the confrontation two nights earlier outside Zhongnanhai. Near the Monument to the People's Heroes, Ren Wanding, a veteran of the 1979 Democracy Wall free-speech movement, read a prepared speech to a squatting and only occasionally-attentive audience. Clutching a sheaf of papers, he tried in vain to make his weak voice carry, stumbling through his address as wind and the din from the Square defeated his efforts.

Ren was speaking on the importance of human rights, a cause for which he had already served four years in jail. Almost incredibly, he had decided to try his luck again, hoping against hope that Deng Xiaoping had acquired more tolerance. In an essay to commemorate the tenth anniversary of Democracy Wall, he had warned that China risked a "whirlwind of discontent" if the system did not change. At the time, it seemed little more than the wishful thinking of a quirky, even pathetic, would-be prophet, living on the frustrated dreams of the past. But the whirlwind which Ren predicted did arrive. It arrived with full force on the very night he chose to speak at Tiananmen Square.

For two days, torrential rain had kept most students penned inside their dormitories. But they had not been idle: they had been organizing. On the evening of Thursday April 20, representatives of 19 Peking colleges had met to form a city-wide unofficial student organisation, the Provisional Action Committee. Late on Friday night, they led tens of thousands of students pouring out of campuses across the city, marching in disciplined ranks towards Tiananmen Square for China's biggest demonstration since the Cultural Revolution.

It was a magical scene. In the darkness, they seemed to come from nowhere, their chants and songs echoing through otherwise deserted streets. Lights flickered on in apartment buildings as people peered out to watch the parade. Late-night buses stopped to let them pass, the passengers leaning from the windows to gaze, smile and sometimes cheer. The students' chants echoed the constant themes of the past week: "Long live democracy ... Down with autocracy ... Down with corruption." There were darker calls for a "liquidation of the blood debt" — a reference to the skirmish with police outside Zhongnanhai. As they approached once more the walls of the leadership compound, they sang the *Internationale*, raising their voices for a deafening chorus. Then, relishing the irony of its opening verse, they broke into the Chinese national anthem: "Rise up, you who refuse to be slaves." Tonight, there would be no unseemly scuffles, no taunting of police. Their order was absolute. Each group of marchers was surrounded by a protective cordon of student marshals, holding hands as they moved along to keep out intruders. Alongside ran organizers, equipped for the first time with loud-hailers and with their ranks displayed on cloth tags dangling from their lapels or on armbands.

The first columns reached Tiananmen Square from the west along Changan Avenue, shortly after midnight. For more than an hour they continued to pour in, more than 100,000 of them in a two-mile-long procession. Every Peking college was represented. So, too, were delegations from Tianjin and other cities. In previous days, the students had shown boldness and initiative, but nothing to suggest the scale or discipline of that night. After reaching the Square, each college took up a predetermined position around the Monument to the People's Heroes with almost military precision. It was as if the Square had suddenly been invaded by an occupying army. Dishevelled and tired, but still remarkably disciplined, the marchers encamped for the night

29

around the university flags and long banners emblazoned with slogans calling for an end to corruption and the autocratic system which they blamed for it. The years of paramilitary training endured by every Chinese student had, it seemed, finally paid off.

AS DAWN approached, it became clear that the students had no intention of leaving before the funeral was over. The affront was monumental, as if 100,000 people had decided to gatecrash the Communist Party's most important social and political event of the year. In side-streets around the Square, security forces began to prepare for action. The students pleaded for compromise. At 5.20, first light, a delegation of three students was received at the steps of the Great Hall by officials from the Funeral Organisation Office. They had three demands: guarantees for the students' safety, permission to pay their last respect before Hu's corpse and a full, official explanation of the police violence in front of Zhongnanhai. At six o'clock, officials gave their reply. Yes, they could guarantee the students' safety, but nothing else. The student leaders thought that this was not enough. They would stay until the funeral service was over.

The minutes ticked by. With only one hour to go before the promised clearing of the Square at eight o'clock, police and soldiers began to pour out of the Forbidden City and the Great Hall of the People. They encircled the entire Square and formed a protective wall of green uniforms in front of the grandly-colonnaded eastern gateway to the Great Hall, overlooking the Square. But they were unarmed. At the last minute, a decision had been taken not to use force.

Shortly before ten o'clock, the leaders began arriving. Deng Xiaoping, Yang Shangkun and other grandees did not deign to face the crowd, but scurried into the Great Hall through side entrances and underground tunnels, shielded like their imperial predecessors from angry subjects. Lesser figures relied on the ten-deep cordon of police and soldiers for protection. An ambulance from the People's Liberation Army General Hospital also stood at the ready, as it always did when the oldest ventured more than a few yards from their oxygen tents, kidney machines and personal nurses. Braving the protesters' chants of "Long live democracy, down with autocracy", the veterans walked slowly up the stone steps, and paused briefly at the top to look down on Tiananmen

Square, a sea of flags and banners. They had not suffered such a rebuke since the dunce's caps and frogmarches of the Cultural Revolution.

Inside the Great Hall, the official funeral ceremony was, by comparison, a pompous and hypocritical sideshow. Zhao Ziyang delivered a glowing eulogy to his deposed predecessor which made no mention of his "errors" or his lax attitude towards "bourgeois liberalisation". Though two of Hu's strongest critics, Chen Yun and Bo Yibo, did not attend, most of the veterans who had stabbed him in the back — including Deng and even the ultra-conservative elder, Wang Zhen — filed reverently past his flag-draped body.

Not everyone in the Great Hall had forgotten how shabbily these same men had treated Hu during the last years of his life. Hu's wife, Li Zhao, was approached by Marshal Nie Rongzhen, the old, wheelchair-bound army veteran, who asked if there was anything he could do to help. She replied: "Yes, clear my husband's name." Television pictures showed her waving Deng away when he tried to offer his condolences. For all its efforts to put on a show of unity, the Party had clearly not healed its old wounds.

When the ceremony ended, many of the leaders chose to leave as they came: through a back entrance. Those who again braved the crowd on Tiananmen Square met with a deafening chorus: "We want dialogue, down with dictatorship." Shouting to make their voices heard above a funeral dirge bellowing from the Square's public address system, the students roared for the prime minister, Li Peng, to come out and listen to their demands. Li had already gone. For two more hours, students kept up their noisy vigil outside the hall until, finally, they decided to leave as they had come, in regimented ranks. Before departing, they made one last gesture of pure theatre. It achieved nothing, but it spoke in a language of symbolism which any Chinese could understand. A trio including Wuerkaixi strode up the steps to the doors of the Great Hall, fell to their knees and raised above their heads a petition addressed to Li Peng calling for dialogue. They were ignored.

CHAPTER FIVE

Deng's editorial

Despite its studied public indifference, the Party leadership had grown obsessed by the students and their demands. Hardliners were pressing for action, saying they wanted an immediate decision on how to respond before Zhao Ziyang, the general secretary, left the next day, Sunday April 23, for an official visit to North Korea. According to the Party's own later account, "comrades in the central leadership" suggested to Zhao that a special meeting be convened on Sunday morning, before his departure by train that afternoon. Instead of accepting the suggestion, "Zhao went golfing as if nothing had happened".

The situation had been exacerbated by rioting at the weekend in two provincial cities. Several thousand people rampaged throughout Saturday in Xian, throwing stones at police and attacking government offices. The trouble, mostly attributed to unemployed youths, began after students had gathered in the centre of the ancient city to watch a televised broadcast of Hu's funeral ceremony. In Changsha, the capital of Hunan, Mao's and Hu's native province, rioters overturned cars and looted shops throughout the night. Again, unemployed workers were held largely to blame. Some of them wore Mao buttons, a sign that they had little in common with the students' struggle for "democracy". But, like the students, they had turned to the past as a way of criticizing the present. They looked back to the Mao era as a time of regular employment and stable prices, a time free from corruption.

The Peking Municipal Party Committee, with the main disorder on its own doorstep, led the pressure for a crackdown on the students. It produced a report describing the student unrest as an "anti-Party and anti-socialist political struggle", which it submitted to an emergency meeting of the Politburo Standing Committee[*] on the night of Monday April 24. The meeting, chaired in Zhao's absence by Li Peng, agreed that the Party *did* face an organized challenge to its authority, and that, to combat the threat, the Politburo should set up "a small group for stopping the turmoil within the central leadership".

By any conventional analysis, the Peking committee and the Politburo Standing Committee had colluded in a most irregular way to by-pass Zhao. But the four men who attended the meeting felt that they had nothing to fear. They knew that Deng Xiaoping had formed the view that the student movement had to be crushed, no matter what the cost: and, in the end, whatever the Party or national constitutions might say, it was what Deng said which mattered.

The next day, Tuesday April 25, Deng issued a secret speech about the "turmoil", copies of which were circulated within the upper levels of the Party. He endorsed the hardline stand, saying "the suggestion of the Peking Municipal Party Committee is correct. The attitude of the Central Committee should be clear ... It is a shame that we have wasted time". For these failings, Zhao, as Party boss, was ultimately responsible. A similar line of attack had been used against Hu in January 1987, also for taking too tolerant a view of student unrest. Deng was also angry at the way Zhao had praised Hu's contribution to Marxism, without mentioning his "mistakes". The "post-mortem evaluation", he said, was "too high".

Deng ordered a "forceful" editorial in *People's Daily* which would condemn the student unrest without equivocation. One already issued on Monday, describing the unrest as a "threat" to China's modernization, had been too weak. "This is not an ordinary student movement, but turmoil," Deng said. "So we must have a clear-cut stand and implement effective measures quickly to oppose and stop this unrest. We cannot let them have their way ... This turmoil is entirely a planned conspiracy to transform a China with a bright future into a China

---

[*]   The five-member "inner circle"

without hope." The aim of the conspiracy, he said, was "to negate the leadership of the Communist Party and the socialist system".

The problem, he said, was not restricted to China. Poland had gone soft, as had the Soviet Union. Concessions would not reduce discontent, but would only fuel it. China would resist. If necessary, blood would be spilled. "We must do our best to avoid bloodshed," he said, "but we should foresee that it might not be possible to completely avoid it ... We need quickly to use a sharp knife to cut the tangled weeds in order to avoid even greater turmoil." He also left little doubt about how the Party could, *in extremis,* enforce its will. "We have several million People's Liberation Army soldiers. What are we afraid of?"

The students lacked copies of the speech, but they knew which way the wind blew. They recognized Deng as their adversary and shed their inhibitions about denouncing him directly. "Though a little dwarf, he grabs great power," read one poster at Peking University. In conversations and even speeches, students demanded openly that he retire. In a subtler vein, they would play on Deng's given name, Xiaoping, which sounded in spoken Chinese very like the words for "small bottle". More than a decade earlier, when Deng was battling radical leftists in the power struggle which followed Mao's death, his supporters among the ordinary people had displayed bottles on window sills and doorsteps. In April 1989, across Peking, bottles were being thrown down to shatter.

By focusing personally on Deng and other leaders, the students found their most potent rallying cry: opposition to corruption. If manual workers and peasants knew or cared little for abstractions like "democracy", they shared a contempt for official greed and privilege. "Under Chairman Mao, cadres had nothing ... Under Deng Xiaoping, cadres are millionaires," ran one popular ditty. Deng's name also appeared at the top of what was probably the most avidly-read and discussed poster of the entire student movement — a list of 27 senior officials, together with the names of their relatives who held privileged positions within the Party, the government, the military and business enterprises. The poster, written in thick black ink on green paper, was called a "revolutionary family tree". It appeared simultaneously on Monday April 24 at both Peking University and the nearby Qinghua University, China's most prestigious scientific college. By displaying the web of nepotism which bound China's leaders, it confirmed what most Chinese already perceived as the real purpose of political power, namely to perpetuate a corrupt and inbred "revolutionary aristocracy", out of touch with the masses.

Deng's wheelchair-bound son, Deng Pufang, was cited as head of the China Welfare Fund for the Handicapped. Much more than just a charity, the fund controlled vast sums of money and had built up an extensive business network in the name of a holding company called Kanghua — mainly, many believed, because of the Deng family connections. Other prominent names included President Yang Shang-kun, whose younger brother[*] Yang Baibing headed the army's General Political Department and whose own son-in-law, Chi Haotian, was head of the General Staff Department.

Though the students focused their anger more on the very old than on the 'younger' leaders, Zhao appeared on the list along with his son, Zhao Dajun, named as president of the Huahai Trading Company in the southern island of Hainan, a by-word for corruption and influence peddling. According to one popular refrain: "Chairman Mao's son went to fight. The sons of Deng Xiaoping and Zhao Ziyang went to buy colour televisions for selling at a profit." Wuerkaixi said of Zhao later: "We must judge him as leader of the Communist Party ... He must bear unshirkable responsibility for the corruption and other mistakes that appeared while he was in charge."

ON SUNDAY April 23, while Zhao golfed and his rivals plotted, the student leaders held their inaugural "congress". Representatives from 21 Peking colleges met amid the ruins of the old Imperial Summer Palace, behind the back entrance to Peking University in the northwest corner of the city. The venue was rich in historical resonance, appropriate to a student movement that professed to be, above all else, patriotic. The palace had been destroyed by British and French troops in 1860, its surviving ruins now symbolizing both foreign aggression and China's own past decadence. It also, perhaps unconsciously, mimicked the circumstances of the Communist Party's own first congress in 1921, held in a park outside Shanghai after police raided the girls' school originally chosen for the event.

---

[*]   Some said cousin.

35

The Peking meeting established a new student body, the Provisional Peking Students Union. Its chairman was Zhou Yongjun, a student from the China University of Politics and Law. Other members included Wuerkaixi and Wang Dan. The impact of the new organisation was immediate. Only a day after its founding, more than 30 Peking colleges ground to a virtual stand-still when students answered its call for a city-wide classroom strike.

By urging students to stay away from lectures, their new leaders hoped to pressure the authorities into agreeing to talks. They wanted an agenda based largely on the seven demands agreed a week earlier in Tiananmen Square. The most profound aim, however, was implicit. "Our purpose was to make the government listen to us and talk to us," said Wuerkaixi later, "that was our only real demand."

Their eyes lifted above their lectures and study books, the students began to look beyond the high walls of their campus compounds. They copied the early years of the Communist Party by forming propaganda teams to spread the word of their cause to ordinary people. Throughout Peking, groups lobbied on street corners, at bus stops and subway stations to drum up support from ordinary residents. They launched a fund-raising drive, fanning out with collection boxes to appeal for donations. The money, they said, would be used to fund an independent student newspaper and the printing of the pamphlets which began to appear on lampposts and walls across Peking explaining their aims.

Within the campuses, the students plastered walls with increasingly strident "big-character posters". Newly-established groups vied for control of public-address systems or set up new ones to combat the stream of propaganda from officially-controlled loudspeakers. Everyone and everything was game for criticism. Leaders were lampooned in cartoons as feudal dictators. Li Peng, previously depicted as a pig, mutated into a snail — "too frightened to come out of his shell".. Party-controlled student unions were condemned as "running dogs". The official Xinhua (New China) News Agency, which had ignored or distorted the student protest, was depicted as a crippled dog with long, ugly teeth. The caption read: "You can't get ivory from dog's teeth."

Some students even dared voice what for 40 years had been the ultimate heresy: that China might have fared better if Chiang Kai-shek, not Mao Tse-tung, had won the civil war. One poster complained that even the maligned Nationalist leader had, in 1931, agreed to meet student delegations from Peking and Shanghai and accept their petitions. "Chiang Kai-shek did not dare ignore the will of the people," said the poster, signed by "a person at Peking University". In a final flourish, the author compared the Communist Party with the emperor of the Qin dynasty[*] who had ordered all books to be burned and had Confucian scholars buried alive. "The age of Qin Shi Huang," it proclaimed, "has now ended."

For the Communist Party, particularly Deng, such signs of disorder and disrespect represented everything it feared most. The Cultural Revolution had begun with a comparably insolent outburst of poster-writing at Peking colleges in 1966. Then, as now, the leaders were attacked both in their own right and through their offspring. Deng could never forget how his own son had been thrown out of a window at Peking University and crippled for life. Nothing would convince him, or his contemporaries who had suffered at least as severely, that such things would not be repeated. How long would it be before Mao's appeal to "bombard the headquarters" rang out once more? How long before their sons and daughters were again being not just insulted, but jailed and maimed?

The older and more nervous members of the leadership seized upon Deng's call for a "clear-cut" response. He had demanded a toughly-worded *People's Daily* editorial. It was ready within hours of his speech. In a break with normal procedure, it was drafted, not by Hu Qili, the Politburo member responsible for propaganda, but by Xu Weicheng, a conservative ideologue and member of the Peking Municipal Party Committee. Hu was suspected of too-close links with the absent Zhao; again, the Peking apparatus had provided a useful stalking horse for the hardline cause.

The editorial marked a crucial point in the evolution of an official response to the student unrest — the point of no return. The hardliners had published their manifesto. So great was judged to be its importance that it was made public before it had been printed in *People's Daily* itself. That, at least, was part of the reason: the other part was more devious. A copy of the proposed text had been sent that same afternoon

---

[*]   221-206 BC

to Zhao Ziyang in North Korea. According to official accounts, Zhao "cabled back, explicitly expressing full agreement with the policy decision made by Comrade Deng Xiaoping". In reality, he was accepting a *fait accompli*. By the time he received the telegram, the text was already being released. At seven o'clock on April 25, it was being read on national television news. It was repeated on national radio and, closer to home, relayed over loudspeakers at Peking's universities throughout the evening.

"This is a planned conspiracy and turmoil," the editorial thundered, repeating almost word for word Deng's judgment. "Its essence is once and for all to negate the leadership of the Communist Party of China and the socialist system. This is a serious political struggle confronting the whole Party and the people of all nationalities throughout the country ... All comrades of the Party and people throughout the whole nation must understand clearly that if we do not resolutely check this turmoil, our State will have no calm days."

After days of confusion and conflicting signals, Emperor Deng had spoken. The Party rushed to distil his wisdom into action. On April 26, the Peking Municipal Party Committee summoned 10,000 cadres to a mass rally in the Great Hall of the People to prepare them for the "grave political struggle" ahead. "We can no longer tolerate this turmoil," warned the Peking Party secretary, Li Ximing, who could now voice his anger publicly after days of private manoeuvring to secure a crackdown. "Our country will be without a peaceful day if we do not resolutely put an end to the turmoil," he told the rally, echoing *People's Daily* and thus Deng. Later in the day, Peking television carried a notice from city authorities: all public gatherings, unauthorized speeches, leaflets and fund-raising efforts were henceforth banned.

In Shanghai, 14,000 Party cadres assembled in a sports stadium to hear the same message and to steel themselves for confrontation against the "tiny handful" who were trying to "poison the minds of the people". Afterwards, the city's Party boss, Jiang Zemin, delivered his own clear signal that Zhao Ziyang, or at least the reform-minded intellectuals he patronized, should consider themselves on the defensive. He ordered the dismissal of Qin Benli, the 70-year-old founding editor of the Shanghai-based *World Economic Herald*, a weekly publication with a reputation for bold and incisive reporting and a liberal editorial line. It had long been a thorn in the side of conservative officials, who resented its frequent attacks on their "feudal" political habits. The time had come, said Jiang, for the situation to be "rectified".

Throughout Wednesday April 26, national radio and television blared diatribes against the student "turmoil". Loudspeakers on university campuses warned that students who continued to march would have to "face the consequences", not only for themselves but also for their fathers and mothers. Many teachers who supported the students' ideals grew increasingly alarmed by the possibility of bloodshed and pleaded with their pupils not to march. Anonymous posters appeared on campus walls suggesting that Fang Lizhi's wife, Li Shuxian, was instigating the student unrest for her own ends. These were unsigned, but their quality — professionally printed rather than scrawled — left little room for doubt that they had been prepared by the authorities, not by students.

Late on the night of Wednesday April 26, police gathered on Tiananmen Square to strip the Monument to the People's Heroes of all the wreaths, posters and banners which had been placed there in the preceding 11 days. The period of mourning for Hu Yaobang was over, Peking authorities announced, removing the alibi which had been the students' principal source of protection.

CHAPTER SIX

A defiant reply

The Communist Party leadership regarded its combination of veiled threats, intimidation and strident propaganda as a tried and tested weapon. Its ferocious public campaigns of isolation and humiliation had invariably silenced and demoralized dissenters; after which they could be punished privately at leisure. But if, for the time being, the Party was concentrating its efforts on a propaganda assault, it was also making contingency plans to back this with force. Deng invoked his authority, as head of the Party's Central Military Commission, to order the movement of 20,000 soldiers of the 38th Army to forward bases around Peking. If the Party faced a "grave political struggle", he wanted to make sure he, not the enemy, had the greater resources. His warning, that it might be necessary to "spill blood", was becoming an ever-less-idle threat.

Among the students, the harsh language of the April 26 editorial engendered not fear, but rage. As soon as the text was made public on the night of April 25, leaders of the newly-formed Provisional Peking Students' Union called a crisis meeting to decide tactics. The following day, they held a rally at the China University of Politics and Law to announce their decision. They would take to the streets the next day, Thursday April 27. They also announced new demands, reducing their original set of seven to three: the government must agree to talk to student representatives on an equal footing, the public security ministry must apologies for the violence the week before in front of Zhongnan-hai, and the Xinhua News Agency and other official media must give fair and accurate coverage to the student movement. To ward off charges that they were trying to overthrow communism and spread turmoil, the student leaders made a skilful course-correction. To the by-now familiar chants of "Long live democracy" and "Down with dictatorship", they added a new slogan: "Support the correct leadership of the Communist Party of China, support Socialism and Reform".

Though the students maintained their outward show of imperturbability, some of them had been privately very shaken by the official propaganda, and questioned the wisdom of provoking the authorities further by marching as planned. The head of the Provisional Students' Union, Zhou Yongjun, was among those counselling caution as fierce arguments broke out between the movement's own "moderates" and "hardliners". Only hours before the march was due to begin, student leaders at Qinghua University announced they had all resigned from the Provisional Union and would not take part in the planned demonstration.

Nervous debate continued on campuses throughout the night, amid rumours that the army was preparing to strike pre-emptively to stop the march before it even started. "We began to accept that it might end in death," said Wuerkaixi. Many students wrote their wills, or what they thought might be their last letters home. At Peking Normal University, the head of the college spent nearly five hours, until three in the morning, trying to persuade Wuerkaixi and his lieutenants not to march.

At Peking University, a makeshift public address system spread a message of defiance. "Comrade Mao Tse-tung was right," one speaker told thousands of students gathered outside. "If you let the people speak, the heavens will not fall down. But if you don't let the people speak, you yourself will fall ... the lessons of history are worth remembering." Wang Dan and other activists were abandoning their headquarters in a rubbish-strewn dormitory. They had decided to spend the night in hiding for fear that they might be kidnapped by the authorities. Behind them, they left a note on the door: "God Protect Us".

But whatever second thoughts students might have had on that sleepless Wednesday night, their fears evaporated on Thursday morning. At twenty to ten, almost two hours later than scheduled, thousands surged out of the main gate of Peking University. Led by a young student in glasses who recited sections from the constitution guaranteeing the right to demonstrate, they set off for Tiananmen.

Only a few thousand strong at the start, they were soon joined by another column of banner-waving students advancing from the north. These had come from Qinghua University, ignoring their own leaders' decision not to march. Within half an hour, the numbers had swelled to an almost unstoppable tide. As they marched through the university district of Haidian, the first police cordons crumpled amid chants from bystanders of "let them through, let them through". Faint-hearted undergraduates, who had initially refused to take part, ran to catch up. Even the Qinghua campus leaders, their decision not to march overturned, decided to accept the will of what they called the "broad masses of the students".

At each junction the procession grew bigger, as tributaries from smaller colleges joined the main flow. Factories and offices along its route came to a standstill as workers in overalls, bureaucrats in jackets and even some Party officials leaned from windows, flashing victory signs or shouting their support. At construction sites, workers in hardhats banged tin lunch-boxes with chopsticks and spoons to urge the students on. Middle-aged spectators gave ice-cream and soft drinks to help the students combat the brilliant sunshine of a beautiful Peking spring.

At its peak, the 14-hour parade was 150,000-strong and covered nearly 25 miles. Cheered all the way by hundreds of thousands of onlookers, the students leading it burst through line after line of paramilitary police to seize virtual control of the centre of Peking.

As their leaders had instructed, they tempered their cries for more democracy with shouts of support for the "correct leadership of the Communist Party". Some even carried banners proclaiming support for Deng's personal creed, the "Four Cardinal Principles" of Chinese-style socialism. If these were meant as totems to ward off the wrath of the Party, the spell appeared to work. Though police made a semblance of trying to halt the march, its resistance was rarely more than token. The troops which Deng had called to the capital never came out in force, and the few who did appear were unarmed. In all probability, there had been no positive decision within the Party leadership to order a "soft line"; rather, the leadership had simply never anticipated so massive a display of defiance and, therefore, the security forces had prepared no tactics. Never before had the displeasure of the Party been quite so easily ignored.

As the march pushed onward, along Changan towards Zhongnanhai and Tiananmen, security forces brought up reinforcements for one last attempt at halting it. They were too slow, and the students poured through a breach in police lines. Crowds of bystanders, who had booed the arriving trucks, now cheered the successful marchers. A convoy of 20 military vehicles filled with soldiers was parked outside the Great Hall of the People. The troops, caught off guard, suddenly found themselves surrounded by a jeering crowd. Anger quickly turned to farce, as it became clear that the troops wanted to do nothing but escape. "The people's army should love the people," the crowd shouted as the trucks gingerly inched away. "Brothers, go home and plough your fields."

From stands at the front of the Forbidden City, beneath the portrait of Mao Tse-tung, officials looked on helplessly as the parade flowed by. Then, the students had one more surprise in store for them: rather than halting to occupy Tiananmen Square, they marched straight on past, chanting and singing as they entered on the homeward leg of their journey. They had made their point. They had conquered Tiananmen. They knew it. The officials knew it. There was no need for further ado. If this was China's "grave political struggle", nobody could doubt the victors of this first round. "It was as if hundreds of thousands of people in Peking had thrown cold water in the faces of the leaders and woken them up," Wuerkaixi commented two days later. "It was a great moment and a great victory."

As the students were marching back to their campuses that Thursday afternoon, Radio Peking carried an urgent announcement from the State Council of senior government ministers. "We are ready to conduct dialogue with the students at any time," an unnamed spokesman announced. The offer was hedged by the admonishment that students should "demand dialogue through the normal channels instead of resorting to extremist actions". But, for the first time, the authorities had thought it prudent publicly to make a concession.

CHAPTER SEVEN

Zhao intervenes

"History will never forget April 27 1989," read the long white banner hanging from a dormitory balcony at Peking University. The mood in campuses across the city was one of triumph. Everything seemed possible. The students had defied the Party. They had articulated popular pressure for reform on a scale which could not be ignored. They had even, by their actions, won at least the hint of a compromise. All this amounted to far more than they might ever have dared hope when they first fluttered paper flowers in memory of Hu Yaobang less than a fortnight before. At another time, the students might have chosen this moment to declare victory, to end their classroom boycott and street protests.

Two historic coincidences, however, sustained them. In a week's time it would be May 4, the day on which, above all others in the year, they should be waving the banners of freedom. Then, less than a fortnight later, they would have the once-in-a-lifetime chance to present their case, not only to the Communist Party of China, but to the world. On May 15, Mikhail Gorbachev, the President of the Soviet Union, would arrive in Peking to begin a four-day visit to China. The pride of the Party, and the attention of world media, offered an enormous source of leverage. "We have the ability to threaten them with further demonstrations," boasted Wuerkaixi — demonstrations which could scarcely be put down in front of the whole world, and which would turn the climax of Deng Xiaoping's political career into an international embarrassment.

The movement, they decided, was invincible. To make their point, they renamed and restructured their organisation. It would no longer be a provisional union but a permanent one. On Friday April 28, representatives now drawn from more than 40 colleges and institutes met at Peking Normal University to found the Autonomous Union of Peking Students, with Wuerkaixi as its chairman. The movement's previous titular leader, Zhou Yongjun, was dropped, a victim of his own pleas for moderation.

If the students were not "invincible", they were certainly stubborn. The leadership, now also looking ahead to the Gorbachev visit and the international scrutiny which that would bring, tried a change of tactics, signalled by another, less strident editorial in the *People's Daily* of April 29. The students were asked, rather than ordered, to return to their classes: "The sooner, the better. Resuming classes in the current situation is a practical way to protect the national interest and maintain stability."

The same appeal was repeated by Yuan Mu, the government spokesman who had been told by Li Peng, the prime minister, to create some acceptable form of "dialogue". Yuan convened a round of talks on Saturday April 29, which won applause within the Party for its elegant stage-management. Most of the 50 students invited to take part were members of official student unions and, as such, had as much interest in halting the unrest as their elders in the Party. Several activists in the Autonomous Students Union were also invited, but not as representatives of the new and still technically-illegal body. Wuerkaixi was asked to join in but stormed out of the building when officials told him to "cool down" before the talks had even begun. "I've been cool all along: now it's up to them," he said after his angry exit.

Yuan's dialogue turned out to be less of a negotiating session than a press conference. Several students aired their grievances about corruption and challenged Yuan to explain why the Party had ousted Hu Yaobang. Yuan acknowledged in return that problems did exist, but evaded promising any solutions more substantial than a halt to the importing of expensive foreign cars for the leaders. One student obligingly complained about politicians who indulged in extravagant pastimes — such as golf, of which Zhao Ziyang was China's best-known fan. The remark, Yuan promised, would be forwarded to the "relevant departments". The "talks", which lasted a little over three hours, were broadcast that same night on national television.

A second set of "talks" followed the next day, Sunday April 30, with officials from the Peking city government and Party apparatus. In another attempt to defuse student anger, Li Ximing, the Party secretary, previously one of the firmest advocates of a harsh crackdown, met one of the students' early demands by disclosing his own and family members' incomes. His monthly wage, he assured them, was only 300 yuan (£45). His son was an "ordinary cadre" while his two daughters held the equally mundane jobs of medical worker and accountant. He left his audience with a warning. "Even though you students do not like to hear the words 'being used by others', I have to remind you that certainly a very few people want your action to throw our country into turmoil," he said. "If this situation is allowed to go unchecked, the consequences would be too ghastly to contemplate."

It was a prophetic warning, but one which the students preferred to ignore. They dismissed the "dialogues" as a sham. "This is like the government talking with the government," said Peng Tuo, a spokesman for the Autonomous Students Union. To have corruption and other issues raised in such a forum was a start. But the real issue, as the students saw it, was that the Party could still not bring itself to acknowledge the organizations created by the students themselves. They decided to step up the pressure.

After a strategy session at Peking Normal University on Tuesday May 2, 65 student activists set off on bicycles to deliver an ultimatum to government and Party officials. Either the officials would agree to the students' terms for talks, or there would be another mass demonstration on May 4. "If the government refuses our conditions, they will have to deal with the biggest demonstrations ever seen in the capital," threatened Wuerkaixi. The students must have known, however, that their conditions would never be met. They wanted official recognition of their Autonomous Union; they refused to open discussions with anyone other than the five members of the Politburo Standing Committee; and in a final flourish of confidence, they demanded a response by noon the following day.

The ultimatum was summarily rejected. Yuan Mu called it "naive and impulsive", adding: "I can see from this that there really are people behind the scenes who are giving the students ideas in an attempt to create social upheaval." Of the students themselves, he said obliquely: "We are not planning to take action against them *yet*. If we take action now, that would be too soon."

TOO soon for what? Though Yuan Mu could scarcely say so, the problem was that it was too soon for the leadership to have agreed on a course of action acceptable to all its members. Though conservatives wanted the crackdown, Yuan could not properly speak for Zhao Ziyang, who had remained publicly silent since his return from Pyongyang on April 30. Privately, Zhao had shown a sympathetic attitude towards the protests which had so profoundly irritated Deng that the latter would not now even speak to him. The remaining question was how Zhao would play his hand in public.

The answer was that Zhao, like the students, was fixated by the powerful, unpredictable forces which Mikhail Gorbachev's arrival threatened to unleash. The visit would be the first by a Soviet leader to Peking in 30 years and the most important diplomatic event since China's restoration of friendly relations with the United States in the early 1970s. It would represent the apparent realization of Deng Xiaoping's vision of China's place in the world: a balanced relationship with both superpowers, achieved almost entirely on China's own terms. Deng had long indicated that he regarded the summit as the last great milestone of his career, the last great problem which he alone could resolve. His retirement, long wielded as a tactical device rather than a sincere intent, might then finally become a reality.

Events suggest that when Zhao arrived back in Peking, he judged that the moment had come to assert his own claim to the succession. He knew that many in the Party, Deng among them, would rather see him follow Hu Yaobang into the wilderness, a scapegoat for the student unrest. But he had sighted a more distant and daring opportunity: that if Deng's policy of coercion were seen to fail, then Deng himself might be the more convenient scapegoat.

Zhao set his course on May 3, when he delivered a speech anticipating the 70th anniversary of the May Fourth Movement to an audience of senior leaders including President Yang Shangkun, Li Peng and other members of the Politburo. He appealed for calm and unity, standard themes that could cause little offence. "If you lose stability," he said, "nothing will be achieved". He even alluded with seeming approval to part of the Deng-inspired *People's Daily* editorial. But while Zhao sounded emollient, the important words of his speech were the ones he omitted to say. He had rejected a request from President

Yang that he make an explicit condemnation of "bourgeois liberalisation". The Old Guard was furious.

The next day, May 4, Zhao made his struggle public. As tens of thousands of students paraded into the centre of the capital, the Asian Development Bank was opening its annual meeting in the Great Hall of the People. Yang Shangkun had agreed to give the opening address, which proved to be an uninspiring discourse on the need for stability. It was quickly forgotten when Zhao arrived in the hall for what had been envisaged as little more than a courtesy visit.

Instead, Zhao delivered the most sensitive speech he would ever make, an address which would be reported around the world and, more importantly, broadcast repeatedly on national television and radio in coming days. The speech would implicitly repudiate the editorial in the *People's Daily* of April 26, which had attacked the student "turmoil" in terms which every member of the Chinese Communist Party knew to have expressed Deng's will. From the point at which Zhao delivered this speech, coexistence with Deng would become impossible.

The drafting of the critical address had been entrusted to Bao Tong, Zhao's closest political adviser and head of the Communist Party's Political Reform Research Centre, a reformist "think-tank". Bao had been keeping his head down for months, out of the way of hardline snipers who complained that he — meaning, by association, Zhao — was too liberal. But the time for such manoeuvring was past. He and Zhao had to make a stand.

Zhao, dressed in a light business suit, looked very much at home among the bankers whom he was addressing. "At the moment," he told them, "student demonstrations are still under way in Peking and some other cities. But, I deeply believe, the situation will gradually calm down. There will be no great turmoil in China. I am very confident of this." The coded sentiments were probably lost on Zhao's immediate audience, but Party members immediately recognized the words as fighting talk. Deng had already declared the student movement to be "turmoil" and had ordered the Party to act accordingly. For Zhao to say that there was, and would be, "no great turmoil" was a straightforward contradiction.

Deng had seen the protest movement as a "planned political conspiracy" designed to "negate, once and for all, the leadership of the Communist Party". Zhao gave the bankers a different story. The students, he said, were "in no way opposed to our fundamental system". He began to sound almost casual. "Of course," he said, "in a country as big as China, it is unavoidable that there will always be some people who hope to see turmoil. There will always be people taking advantage." The protests had mushroomed, he suggested, not because of any "conspiracy" but because of "imperfections in the socialist legal system and democratic supervision and lack of openness in the system of work". While the bankers listened with polite indifference, Zhongnanhai shuddered beneath the bombshells.

"It was a turning point," Yang Shangkun later fumed at a meeting of the Party's Military Commission. "It entirely exposed the different opinions of the Politburo Standing Committee." The unity of the Party, he said, had been betrayed. It was speaking with "two different voices". According to Yang, Zhao had started pressing for a reassessment of Deng's treasured April 26 editorial on the very day that he arrived back in Peking from North Korea. "He wanted the 'Party Centre'[*] to toe his line and to declare the editorial wrong." Now, Zhao had gone it alone.

FOR THE students, outside in Tiananmen Square, the May 4 march was another triumph. Seventy years to the day after their pioneering predecessors, they commemorated the anniversary of the May Fourth Movement on their own terms — not as a celebration of the planting of the seeds of communism, but as a reminder of how little progress had been made towards fulfilling those first calls for "science and democracy". Tens of thousands had again bulldozed their way through police lines. Once in Tiananmen, they planted the blue and white flag of the independent student union on the Monument to the People's Heroes. Better still, the cause had been taken up for the first time by an organized group other than students — some 300 journalists from *People's Daily* and dozens of other official publications, who cheered the parade down Changan Avenue. One of the rocks of the Communist Party's authority, its control of the media, had begun to crumble.

---

[*]   The apparatus of the national Party leadership

But the scene on the Square later that day offered a more subdued picture. Successful as the students had been, fatigue was starting to take its toll. It had been a big demonstration, but not, as Wuerkaixi had hoped, the biggest ever. The numbers had shrunk since the previous Thursday; the tension of the previous week had diminished; the strident editorials had ceased; the threat of a confrontation and the danger of bloodshed had receded. Uncertain about where to go next, they were in a mood to be placated.

Zhao's conciliatory tone and implicit rejection of the April 26 editorial found a ready audience. The Autonomous Student Union voted that evening to end its 11-day classroom boycott, a decision which precipitated a major split within the student movement. Wuer-kaixi and several others "resigned" temporarily from their posts. They did so because "there were problems with their analysis", said Wang Zhixin, the 21-year-old secretary general of the Autonomous Union and a leading advocate of a more moderate stand. Many students felt disappointment and disillusionment. "The government's strategy of being neither hard nor soft worked well and now students are not so excited any more," said Ni Xu, another who resigned in disgust. "The authorities are like a cotton pillow: no matter how hard you punch them, they can regain their shape. Here in Peking, the main protest is over."

CHAPTER EIGHT

The hunger strike

If there was ever a time at which China's students and its Party leadership might have found a compromise to end the protests, it was in the week after May 4. Moderate voices had prevailed, it seemed, both inside Zhongnanhai and in Room 400 at Peking Normal University, the dingy dormitory decorated with pin-ups of sultry Chinese pop stars which had become the nerve-centre of the student movement.

Students across the city were drifting back to class. Though two campuses, Peking University and Peking Normal, resisted the back-to-class appeal, their militancy seemed out of place. Other colleges felt that they had done enough for now. "The main thing we have done is to create an atmosphere," said Wang Zhixin, the student organizer. "We have brought the word democracy into the lives of the people of China ... and given them new confidence in criticizing the government." They could also claim another, more tangible, achievement. On Friday May 5, the day after their anniversary march, they finally made it on to the front pages of China's newspapers. *People's Daily*, which only a week before had denounced the student movement as a "planned conspiracy", gave it something close to an official blessing. It published a picture of the students' — illegal — May 4 protest, side-by-side with a photograph of a Communist Youth League gathering to mark the same event. The newspaper also published its first reasonably accurate news story about what the students had been doing.

Other papers were even bolder. Instead of relying on the curt dispatches of the Xinhua News Agency — which grossly underestimated the size of the May 4 march at 20,000 — they printed often-lengthy comments by their own staff, highly sympathetic to the students' cause. The *China Youth News*, one of the more adventurous of China's daily newspapers, quoted the students' own criticisms of earlier official attacks on their movement and of press censorship in general. "We are citizens and the government is dealing with citizens, not children," said one.

The new openness was made possible by Zhao's intervention. "There is no big risk in opening up a bit by reporting the demonstrations and increasing the openness of news," he told the two Central Committee members responsible for propaganda, Hu Qili and Rui Xingwen, on May 6. "Confronted with the will of the people at home and the progressive trend worldwide, we can only guide our actions according to circumstances."

Even Li Peng, the prime minister, felt constrained to adopt the new vocabulary of tolerance rather than disagree openly with Zhao. When he, too, addressed the Asian Development Bank on May 5, he said that dialogue with the students was necessary and would continue. "With our positions basically identical, mutual understanding can be enhanced through more dialogue," he said. "The government hopes that the unrest will calm down."

Convinced that real dialogue was about to begin, the students formed yet another organisation, the Peking Students' Union Dialogue Representative Group. This group, representing 24 Peking colleges, submitted a fresh petition asking for talks and demanding a reply by Monday May 8. It dispensed with the shopping list of 12 preconditions which had accompanied its previous petition on May 2, substituting just two: that the dialogue must be broadcast live on radio and television and that the students should select their own representatives. The proposed agenda would include official recognition of the student movement, a retraction of the April 26 *People's Daily* editorial and the future of the nation's reform programme.

When the May 8 deadline arrived, the students' demands had been neither rejected nor accepted. Their representatives were told by officials that both the government and the Party wanted "broad contacts with the workers, peasants, intellectuals, students and people with non-Party affiliations", but the key demand for recognition of their independent organisation was not addressed. The leadership was dancing around the issue, unable to make a clear statement because of the divisions in its ranks.

While the pre-talks-talking dragged on, some of the more radical student leaders — including Wuerkaixi — cast around for fresh issues on which to focus protest. They seized upon a petition submitted by 1,013 editors and reporters demanding talks about censorship and about the firing of Qin Benli, editor of the *World Economic Herald*. They attempted to stage a protest march in sympathy, but attracted no more than a few hundred students for a rally outside the offices of *People's Daily*. The following day, they held a further, and more imaginative, demonstration against press censorship, bicycling around the city to the offices of the main national media — *People's Daily*, *Guangming Daily*, the Xinhua News Agency, the Central People's Broadcasting Station and the Central Television Station. Despite its novelty value, the protest again failed to attract anything like the support seen in previous weeks. No more than 5,000 students took part and, rather than winning applause from ordinary residents, they met with indifference or irritation as their bicycles snarled up traffic for miles around.

Zhao's conciliatory approach appeared capable of producing the result which the Party wanted: a waning of the student fervour. Superficially at least, his reputation was correspondingly boosted. Across the country, newspapers praised his tolerant stand, quoting students and intellectuals who said that they had been encouraged by his remarks and believed real political reform was in the offing. Hu Jiwei, a former editor of the *People's Daily* and a member of the National People's Congress Standing Committee, described Zhao's conciliatory comments to the Asian Development Bank as a "cause for joy". Yan Jiaqi, China's leading political scientist, hailed the Party boss for "having grasped the crux of the matter" — that the student protest had arisen because of dissatisfaction with the state of Chinese democracy and of the legal system.

Zhao pressed ahead. May 8 marked his third public appearance in five days. Speaking to a delegation of Turkish politicians, he again described the students in sympathetic terms. They had, he said, raised problems which "must be resolved". China, he promised, would "not only push forward with economic reforms but ... also carry forward political restructuring to allow the two concepts to support each other".

Many found Zhao's outspokenness confusing. For his critics, it was simply intolerable. The Peking Municipal Party Committee, already angered and humiliated by the sudden rejection of the hard line which it had pioneered, led the backlash. The city's Party boss, Li Ximing, and its mayor, Chen Xitong, issued an internal document advising

Peking cadres that Zhao's comments to the Asian Development Bank reflected his own views rather than those of the Party as a whole. City officials demanded a meeting with Zhao to voice their complaints. That same day, they presented their case at a special meeting which preceded an enlarged Politburo meeting. Chen Xitong said afterwards that the encounter descended into angry squabbling because Zhao "refused to listen". When told that his remarks contradicted the spirit of the *People's Daily* editorial dictated by Deng, Zhao is said to have snapped: "I'll bear responsibility, if I have made incorrect remarks." The Politburo meeting, two days later, also ended in bickering.

THE BEHAVIOUR of the Peking Municipal Party Committee during this period would ordinarily have constituted gross insubordination. Though they ran Peking, Zhao — at least in theory — ran the country. But as Zhao knew, the Peking committee had powerful backers "behind the curtain". Those backers, though in no sense a formal group, centred on a half-dozen veterans led by Deng. They had begun meeting secretly, probably also on May 8, to define their own response to the student movement. None was a member of the Politburo, none held a cabinet post, none was under 80 years old. All had known one another through decades of social contact and professional rivalry. They were among the last surviving veterans of the generation which had come to power with Mao and were, they thought, the only true guardians of Mao's revolution.

The principal members of Deng's loose-knit group were Wang Zhen, Peng Zhen, Chen Yun and Li Xiannian, and Deng Yingchao (who was not related to Deng Xiaoping). For the past five years, Deng Xiaoping had been at odds with them, trying to enforce their retirement from active politics in order to clear the way for his own protégés. "Even if heaven should fall," he said in 1984, "Hu and Zhao can support it". But his inability to devolve power had put paid to such newer loyalties. Now Hu had gone, and Zhao had spoken against him. He turned back to the handful of survivors who, despite his own efforts, had remained at his right hand. "It has turned out in our favour," he later remarked without apparent irony. "We still have a large group of veterans who have experienced many storms, and have a thorough understanding of things."

Though Deng had relinquished his seats on the Politburo and the Central Committee, he had retained the chairmanship of the Party's Central Military Commission — a post which, subsequent events would prove, was of more than ceremonial value. Wang Zhen, 81, had retired as deputy chief-of-staff of the People's Liberation Army, after a lifetime of battlefield commands. Peng Zhen, 86, had been mayor of Peking until the Cultural Revolution, of which he had been an early victim. After Mao's death, he returned to power as chairman of the National People's Congress. Despite their age, Deng Xiaoping, Wang and Peng were all in remarkably good health. Chen Yun, 84, was so frail that he had not appeared in public since the spring of 1988 and moved around in a wheelchair. For all his frailty, though, he remained one of the most powerful figures in the country. He headed the Party's Central Advisory Commission, which had been conceived as a means of pensioning-off the old, but which continued to wield tremendous influence behind the scenes. Li Xiannian, at least 80, was China's former president. Deng Yingchao was the widow of Chou En-lai, Mao's premier, and the adoptive mother of Li Peng, the prime minister.

A confidential Party circular, issued later to senior cadres, said the group's agenda had turned on a single question: did the Party stand by Deng's hardline editorial in *People's Daily* on April 26? "If we retreat from our judgment, where do we draw the line?" Deng asked his octogenarian colleagues. With one voice, they answered that there could be no retreat. The editorial had assumed an almost mystical importance. Its repudiation would seriously undermine Deng, perhaps thus signalling the end of his own generation's rule. As President Yang Shangkun, himself at least 82, would later explain: "Retreating would be *our* downfall, the downfall of the People's Republic of China." Confirmed in his judgement, Deng planned for its implications. Several times in the course of May, he was said to be in the central Chinese city of Wuhan, meeting privately with the commanders of China's seven military regions to knit them into his battle-plan.

AS THE Party set its shadowy face against compromise, so too did the students. Though their momentum had faltered after May 4, the calendar was on their side. Mikhail Gorbachev would soon be in Peking. On May 12, three days before Gorbachev's arrival, their leaders decided to stage a hunger strike in Tiananmen Square. The tactic had first been suggested in the "Open Letter to Peking Colleges" published immediately after Hu Yaobang's death. Whether it should be used, and whether it would work, however, had been hotly debated. Wang Dan and Wuerkaixi both expressed reservations, doubting that it would be effective. Chai Ling, a 23-year-old psychology student from Peking Normal University, and her husband, Feng Congde, believed it was the decisive weapon. At first, Chai Ling recalled: "We had only 40 hunger strike volunteers. I was heartbroken ... But I went out and spoke to crowds of students at Peking University. By the next day the number had grown to 400."

Before setting off for the Square, the volunteers were treated to a farewell banquet by a group of sympathetic young teachers at Peking University. Wearing white headbands marked "hunger strike" and "democracy warrior", they gulped down plates of food and — a special treat — bottles of beer and *Maotai* sorghum spirit. The meal over, they headed off by bicycle to Peking Normal University to meet other volunteers rallied by Wuerkaixi. From there, they paraded on foot to Tiananmen, arriving to applause from a crowd of supporters already gathered near the Monument to the People's Heroes. Standing in front of the obelisk, amid a sea of banners, Wuerkaixi administered a ceremonial oath. Each hunger striker vowed not to eat until two conditions had been met: "substantive, concrete and equal" dialogue with the leadership and official acknowledgment that the student movement was "patriotic and democratic".

Wang Dan tried to go further. He announced a ban, not only on food but on cigarettes. Even for the most determined hunger strikers, however, this proved too much. Wang retreated. Smoking, he announced a few minutes later, would be permitted. The about-turn captured the mood of the moment: drama, tinged with good-natured farce.

Settling down for a long stay, the thousand hunger strikers made their encampment in the middle of Tiananmen Square. They covered the very spot at which, in two days' time, Yang Shangkun and a military honour guard were due formally to welcome Mikhail Gorbachev to Peking. Sitting and sprawling on spread-out newspapers, the hunger strikers were protected by an outer ring of several thousand, non-fasting students. In the middle of the gathering stood a placard which read: "Hunger Strike Manifesto", a melodramatic document shot through with a shrewd grasp of politics.

"In this sunny, brilliant month of May," ran the manifesto, "we are going on a hunger strike. During this most beautiful moment of youth, we have no choice but to put the beauty of life behind us ... We do not want to die. We would like to lead a good life, because we are in the prime of our lives. We do not want to die. We would like to study hard. Our country is very poor. We will be leaving our country behind if we die. Death is certainly not our goal. But if the death of one person or a group of few would ameliorate lives of a larger group of people and succour the prosperity of our country, we would not have the right to escape death ... Our country has already reached a stage at which prices are soaring, official profiteering is rife, the mighty tower above, bureaucrats are corrupt, many of those with lofty ideals are lost and social order grows worse by the day. At this crucial point of life and death for our race and nation, compatriots, every compatriot with a conscience, please listen to our plea."

In a country where mass starvation had occurred within living memory, where food had only just ceased to be precious, the spectacle of ritualized hunger was an emotive one. The students captured the popular imagination with a force which they had not foreseen and, in doing so, they brought themselves and their cause to a crisis.

For it was both the strength and the weakness of the students that they had created a genuinely "popular" movement, which rose and fell according to the spontaneous support which it attracted in the campuses and on the streets. They were neither initiated nor controlled by a faction within the leadership — however difficult it might be for the leadership itself to accept this fact. As Wuerkaixi later said: "Our movement had absolutely nothing to do with the Party struggle. We didn't care anything for their internal struggles. We wanted to found a new democratic system in China; there was no (leadership) faction supporting a democratic system. Our goal was not to play with the current system. We wanted to rock the system."

Nonetheless, reversing the equations, the Party struggle had everything to do with the student protests. In April, Deng had advocated a hard line. Its apparent failure had created the opportunity for Zhao to advocate conciliation. Now, after a hiatus which had worked to Zhao's advantage, the demonstrations were growing once again. Zhao's softer line was now being discredited, and at a much more sensitive time. If

Zhao could not find a way of clearing the Square before Gorbachev's arrival on Monday, he would be in serious trouble.

Zhao ordered a series of dramatic, last-minute appeals over the weekend. Where Deng had tried to bully the students, Zhao tried to reason with them. "Every patriotic Chinese citizen should safeguard the dignity of the motherland and its international image," he told a meeting of workers inside the Great Hall of the People on Saturday May 13. "It is unreasonable for students or other citizens who have complaints ... to obstruct international relations." Yuan Mu repeated the theme on behalf of the government. "I am sure," he said, "that students will act in a sober-minded and rational way, obey orders and exercise restraint."

The students did nothing of the sort. Their eyes fixed on the prospect of Gorbachev's arrival and the bargaining power which it gave them, they seemed unconcerned by what might happen after it was over. "As for whether we will disrupt Gorbachev's visit," Wang Dan told a crowd of reporters and students on the steps of the Museum of Chinese Revolutionary History, "that is now completely in the hands of the government."

Late on Saturday came a new promise of "dialogue". Xinhua News Agency announced that senior government officials would make themselves available on the Monday. When the students were unmoved, and the hunger strike continued to grow by the hour, the government said it would bring the talks forward to Sunday, the day before Gorbachev's arrival. That afternoon, a van drove into Tiananmen Square to take Wuerkaixi, Wang Dan, Chai Ling and other student leaders to the Party's United Front Department, located in a courtyard across the road from Zhongnanhai. Inside the building, they were met by Yan Mingfu, a Central Committee member close to Zhao Ziyang, and Li Tieying, chairman of the State Education Commission. Yan pleaded with them to leave the Square. As a compromise, he suggested they should not necessarily stop their hunger strike but simply move it to another location, away from Tiananmen and thus away from Gorbachev's view. He even offered an apology — a courtesy for which he would later lose his job. "With regard to dialogue with students, we have not taken measures that should have been taken," he said. "This is our fault."

By seven o'clock in the evening, Yan was on the verge of tears. He made one last appeal. "If you insist on dividing the Party Centre into factions, then you should see that your action is very harmful to the reform faction ... Comrade Zhao Ziyang's intention will be very difficult to carry out. It will be very difficult for comrades working at the forefront." If anything, the pleading only strengthened the students' determination. "The government tried everything to defeat us," Chai Ling would comment later, "but we held our resolve." An appeal from twelve leading scholars and academics widely admired for their outspokenness was spurned. So, too, was a late night visit to Tiananmen Square, only hours before Gorbachev's arrival, by Chen Xitong, Li Ximing and other Peking officials.

By Sunday night, the hunger strikers were 2,000 strong. Tens of thousands had poured into Tiananmen to show support. So far from being the venue for an august state occasion meant to confirm China's standing in the world, the Square had been transformed into a chaotic celebration of defiance and popular contempt for the leaders whom Gorbachev was due to meet. In place of Soviet and Chinese flags, there billowed the colours of dozens of Peking colleges and banners daubed with pro-democracy slogans. The students set up their own loudspeaker system to broadcast speeches and messages in competition with the government's propaganda. The students recognized that their movement had reached its apex. They demanded absolute satisfaction: the immediate, explicit repudiation of the April 26 editorial, and official recognition of their illegal students' union. Otherwise, they pledged, China's leaders would lose face in front of the entire world.

For form's sake, Peking's Public Security Bureau again announced — as it had before Hu Yaobang's funeral and before the May 4 demonstration — that Tiananmen Square would be closed throughout the following day. It ordered everyone present to leave by three o'clock in the morning. The deadline passed unremarked and no police arrived. Shortly after dawn, as the plane carrying Gorbachev left the Siberian city of Irkutsk for Peking, a group of men appeared on the roof of the Great Hall of the People to survey the chaotic scene on the Square beneath them. One of them, dressed in a light Mao suit, took a long look through binoculars. It was Zhao Ziyang. He had failed.

CHAPTER NINE

The Summit

As the Aeroflot Ilyushin jet carried Mikhail Gorbachev over Mongolia towards Peking, its radio crackled with warnings about the extraordinary scenes which lay ahead. Soviet advance-men had been in Tiananmen Square all morning. Their reports, relayed via Moscow, sounded barely credible. "How *big* is this Square?," asked the amazed Gorbachev after being told that hundreds of thousands were converging on the very spot designated for his official welcome.

A week previously, Soviet foreign ministry officials had gingerly suggested to the Chinese that perhaps they might want the visit postponed. The answer was no. The diplomatic event of the decade, the first Sino-Soviet summit in 30 years, would go ahead as planned. But as Gorbachev must have known long before his plane touched down at noon on Monday May 15, planning would have little to do with it.

The welcoming ceremony was hastily switched from Tiananmen to the old Peking airport. There had not even been enough time to lay a red carpet; the ceremony lasted barely 10 minutes. Accompanied by President Yang Shangkun, Gorbachev briskly reviewed an honour guard and received a 21-gun salute. Flustered Soviet officials distributed copies to journalists of the speech which he had drafted, but not delivered. They pondered his choice of theme: "We have come to China in spring time — the good season of burgeoning nature and the awakening of new life. All over the world, people associate this season with renewal and hope."

They were certainly doing that in Tiananmen Square. Drenched in brilliant sunlight, it had become a giant canvas of defiance, an eastern Woodstock. The hard core of students had been camping out for three days. The crowd had dropped to about 20,000 shortly before dawn but had risen back to more than 100,000 by noon. Throughout the afternoon, it continued to grow. Teachers, factory workers, writers and junior school students paraded into the centre of Peking. For the first time since the student protests began exactly a month before, the general public was no longer merely cheering from the sidelines, but joining in. Groups criss-crossed the Square, chanting slogans and singing songs, sometimes to mock, sometimes to inspire, as when they roared the *Internationale* or the stirring songs of the civil war.

The mood was anarchic but oddly gentle, despite some vigorous pushing and shoving when armed police moved in to clear two streets behind the Great Hall of the People. Amid the smiling and laughing, the hunger strikers served notice that the underlying purpose was indeed serious. "Mother, we like food but we like democracy even more," read a tattered banner. Another: "Our children are going hungry, Deng Xiaoping. What are your children doing?" Through the songs and chants cut the sirens of ambulances, slicing through the turmoil to take students, weak from hunger and exhaustion, off to hospital. By the end of the day, more than 50 had been carted away, though most returned to the Square as soon as they had recovered. Medical orderlies in white coats kept a constant watch on the hunger strike area, administering glucose and water.

Above the multitude, on a flagpole where the hammer and sickle should have flown, fluttered a large banner scrawled with the words "hunger strike". But the Soviet leader had not been forgotten. Banner after banner hailed his arrival. "Welcome the initiator of *glasnost*," read one written in Russian; "Democracy our common ideal," another. "In Moscow they have Gorbachev, who do we have in China?" ran a common refrain; "We need *perestroika*, too." Gorbachev's portrait had taken the place of Hu's looking out across the Square, in an unmistakable rebuke to the Chinese leaders whom the students were measuring against him.

Gorbachev saw none of it. He spent most of his first day in the Diaoyutai (Fishing Platform) State Guest House and at the Soviet Embassy. At four in the afternoon, he was due to meet Yang at the Great Hall of the People. Ordinarily, he would have swept in through the grand eastern entrance overlooking Tiananmen Square. But, with the way now blocked, his motorcade followed backstreets from the Soviet ambassador's residence, past the Oriental Restaurant, a ramshackle warehouse and a long row of grey courtyard homes to arrive at a narrow

61

back-gate on the west side of the hall. Two soldiers saluted raggedly as the motorcade careered past a pile of rubble and halted by a disused basketball court. Perched on the back seat of his Zil, Gorbachev could be seen peering out of the window down the one street in the area still controlled by the authorities. At the end of it, behind a row of paramilitary police, jostled a crowd of demonstrators.

Gorbachev had arrived shortly after six o'clock, two hours behind schedule. Pressed to explain the long delay, a Soviet minion offered a single phrase: "Comrade Gorbachev has been resting." He would do a lot more resting in the days which followed, as his trips to the Forbidden City and a Peking Opera house were cancelled and his press conference was moved at the last minute from the Great Hall to his own guest house. Discretion, however, continued to be the watchword of his party. On the final day, Gennady Gerasimov, his spokesman, allowed that traffic conditions had been "a little strange".

In his exchanges with Yang, Gorbachev referred delicately to the student cause. "We have grown smarter," he said, "and the next generation will be smarter yet." What was needed, he said, was "a sensible balance between the generations — the energy of the young people, speaking out against conservatism, and the wisdom of the older generation." Yang replied: "We feel that our speed is too fast; it should be reduced a little."

A similar nicety was apparent at the evening's banquet, hosted by Yang. The curtains along the gallery within the Great Hall of the People, usually drawn back to reveal a panorama of Tiananmen Square, had been closed. Gorbachev delivered a toast. "Today," he said, "we have been able to see some architectural ensembles, to drive through the streets of the capital and meet its people. What impressed us most was their openness and friendliness." Yang was equal to the moment. "It has not been easy for us," he confided, "to create a situation in which the leaders of our countries have been able to hold these historic meetings."

LIKE a Shakespearean sub-plot, near-farcical efforts were still being made behind the scenes to persuade the students to leave Tiananmen and restore to the leadership a fig leaf of dignity. Zhao Ziyang told his loyal supporters, Yan Mingfu and Li Tieying, to call another meeting with student leaders. It was fruitless.

At midnight, the Central Committee General Office issued another plaintive plea. Broadcast to students at ear-splitting volume through loudspeakers on Tiananmen Square, it begged them to "please go back to school ... The Party and government are studying reasonable suggestions and demands raised by the broad masses of students and will take feasible measures and steps to resolve the questions". It said that the Standing Committee of the National People's Congress would meet in June to discuss "crucial questions which are the concern of the masses, and resolve them by promoting democracy and building up the legal system". Like all the promises made that week, it was ignored by the students at the time, and forgotten by the leadership not long after.

The formal climax of Gorbachev's visit came at four minutes past ten the next morning, when, in the Fujian Room of the Great Hall of the People, he shook hands with Deng Xiaoping. Thirty years of estrangement between Moscow and Peking had come to an end. But even Gorbachev's mind was probably wandering from the secular equations of global politics to more immediate circumstances. He had been up late the night before, after his banquet with President Yang, summoning Soviet journalists who had been out among the crowds, his China experts and resident Soviet diplomats to try to explain what was going on behind the curtains his hosts had drawn so tightly around him.

If he had hoped for elucidation from Deng, he was disappointed. The Chinese leader dwelt on grander issues of world affairs. It was, Soviet officials said later, a rambling discourse, in which could be detected Deng's irritation at past Soviet "aggression" and China's loss of territory. "Although Chairman Deng's views are not groundless," Gorbachev responded politely, "the Soviet side has some different views." When the conversation moved to Marxism, the two agreed that adjustments had to be made if each country wished to modernize. "The way we adapt to these conditions will determine the influence of socialism in the world," Gorbachev said. "We are following with keen interest what is happening in China and have learned what is helpful to us."

Gorbachev's curiosity about the protests was not disinterested. If the Soviet Union was to learn anything from China, and if it was to deal effectively with China in the future, it would first have to know what pressures were bearing on its leaders and how they intended to react. He was not alone in his confusion. Even Li Peng seemed at this point to be wavering from his previous hard line — though, equally, he might for form's sake have been attempting simply to present a stance compatible with that of Zhao. "We don't think that freedom, democracy and human rights are a monopoly of the capitalist countries. People in socialist countries should also enjoy freedom, democracy and sufficient human rights," he told Gorbachev. "China is prepared to improve these aspects in its political reform."

The most revealing encounter for Gorbachev came when he met Zhao. Though the other meetings had gone well enough, only with Zhao did he feel truly at ease. Meeting for the first time, the two spent most of their time discussing what Zhao called the "critical period" of socialist reform. Gorbachev saw Zhao's troubles as a possible harbinger of his own. "I am sure you will sort out this problem yourselves to the benefit of your people," Gennady Gerasimov quoted him as saying. "We too have our hotheads who want to renovate socialism overnight but that is impossible. It does not happen in real life, only in fairy tales."

Towards the end of their conversation, Zhao made what seemed to be a modest off-the-cuff comment, almost a truism. He told Gorbachev that, though he held the title of general secretary, it was Deng Xiaoping, not himself, who was the Party's "helmsman". "The whole Party knows," he said, "that we cannot do without him, without his wisdom and experience." He went on to say that a resolution had been passed by the Central Committee in 1987: "On the most important questions, we still need (Deng) as the helmsman". Zhao added a footnote, for Gorbachev's benefit: "This information has never been published for the outside world until today." It was a sensational departure from the hermetic practices of Chinese politics. Zhongnanhai was in uproar. This was no ingenuous tribute to Deng, said Zhao's rivals: rather, it was an attempt to shift on to him the blame for China's political troubles, revealing a state secret *en route*. "Comrade Zhao Ziyang used the opportunity of meeting Gorbachev," the Party later declared, "deliberately to direct the fire of criticism at Comrade Deng Xiaoping and to make the situation even worse." The meeting with Gorbachev was Zhao's last known official engagement.

THE STUDENTS did not need Zhao to tell them who was really running China. "Deng Xiaoping should retire," read one of many banners criticizing the now-revealed helmsman. "Down with the emperor," many chanted. They also mocked Li Peng's reticence: "Missing for a month: the prime minister of China", read a placard mocked-up as a police missing-person notice.

Just as Gorbachev had mobilized the students, the hunger strike had mobilized Peking, providing a focus for every imaginable grievance. The symbolism could not have been more potent: China's rulers had become so isolated, so stubborn, so proud, that rather than talk with a group of young students, they would prefer to let them die. On Tuesday, not tens, but hundreds of thousands poured into Tiananmen in a tidal wave of sympathy for the hollow-eyed, exhausted fasters. Among them were students from the provinces, who had revived the Cultural Revolution practice of travelling without tickets. Almost 60,000 arrived in this fashion at Peking railway station during Gorbachev's stay.

The Monument to the People's Heroes now looked more like a military field hospital than a student sit-in. In this fourth foodless day, 600 were taken to hospital after fainting or suffering hallucinatory fits. Others endured severe diarrhoea after drinking unclean water stored in large plastic drums.[*] With the students' borrowed ultimatum of "give me liberty or give me death" now looking more credible, the Peking Union Medical College and several hospitals were called in to set up emergency treatment centres. Dozens of students, motionless inside canvas tents or under plastic sheeting, received salt and water solutions through intravenous drips. At the northwest corner of the Square, a dozen students from the Peking Drama Institute began refusing not only food but water, too. The only fluid they accepted was the occasional dab from a wet cloth on the cheeks and forehead. Lying completely still, each had a red rose on his neck — a coffin-like pose that reduced even the most boisterous onlookers to quiet murmuring of concern. Behind them, a huge tableau had been painted with two, writhing naked figures separated by the legend: "Save the People".

---

[*]   Wuerkaixi, though a hunger-striker, was secretly eating noodles at night in the back seat of a car, bending low to hide his face. Such a breach of discipline was necessary, he explained to a friend, because as a "leader" he needed to conserve his strength, and because he suffered from a heart condition. His lapse was kept secret. Official propaganda later made great play of a film showing Wuerkaixi banqueting in the Peking Hotel: but this was taken long after the hunger-strike had ended.

65

With serious illness and death on the Square a real possibility, Yan Mingfu resumed his attempts at appeasement. Coming on to the Square for the first time, he shouted hoarsely: "You can reserve the right to protest. But you have no right to ruin your health, because your health belongs to the future of China." He offered himself as a "hostage" against the Party's assurance that it would not punish protesters. "Your spirit and bravery have moved people throughout the nation," he said. Amid mingled applause and heckling, Yan left.

The students had been joined by organized groups of supporters from all sections of society. Journalists from *People's Daily* carried a banner reading: "Support the students who dare to speak the truth." A contingent arrived from the Party's Liaison Department, responsible for supervising links with parties abroad — including, as of that afternoon, that of the Soviet Union. Staff of the official All-China Federation of Trade Unions handed out leaflets calling for reform of unions to allow greater autonomy: "Trade unions should work and speak for the workers and masses."

Across the Square from the Great Hall of the People, as Deng and Gorbachev were shaking hands, staff of the Museum of Chinese Revolutionary History dangled from the roof a giant banner bearing a V-for-victory sign. "Talk to the students, talk to the students," chanted a group of engineers and technicians from the Ministry of Petroleum. A band of young blue-collar workers paraded under the banner "City People's Support Group". Schoolchildren shouted: "If you fall, there will still be us to take over." As a handbill distributed by the students proclaimed with more than a hint of pride: "The Communist Party's own backyard has caught fire."

That night, after his meeting with Gorbachev, Zhao issued a statement in the name of all five members of the Standing Committee of the Politburo, saluting the Tiananmen Square encampment. "Your patriotic spirit in calling for democracy and law, opposing corruption and promoting reform is commendable," it said. It promised that the government would not punish them at a later date. It also pledged to "propose and adopt concrete measures to enhance democracy and law, oppose corruption, build an honest and clean government and expand openness". It was hard to say whether the students were shrewd or stupid in their reaction to the statement. They ignored it. They were not interested in long-term promises, however seemingly benign and unqualified these might be. They wanted something much more immediate and much more specific: a repudiation of the April 26 editorial; in effect, an *ad hominem* repudiation of Deng, which even Zhao could not give.

The following day, Wednesday, the students staged their biggest demonstration yet. At their encouragement, more than a million people took to the streets. They did so again on Thursday, the day that Gorbachev left for Shanghai. Sympathy demonstrations broke out in at least 24 cities across the country. Along Changan, hotel bell-boys in pink dinner jackets turned out alongside Mao-suited cadres from the foreign ministry. The national volleyball team was there and so was a Christian seminary, marching under the banner: "The Lord Loves You. Long Live Democracy." Shaven-headed Buddhist monks paraded in yellow robes. Schoolchildren thrust tiny fists into the air, led by their teachers in chants of "long live democracy, down with corruption". Workers arrived from the Peking Brewery, the Capital Iron and Steel Works and the Peking Jeep Corporation. "Get up and stand up for your rights," chanted a group of teenagers, carrying a black and white banner bearing the image of Bob Marley, the Jamaican reggae star. Even the KGB was swept up in excitement. One group of heavy-set Soviet security guards, stranded in a huge traffic jam near the Great Hall of the People, flashed victory signs from the window of their Lada car. Only when the car's radiator overheated and began billowing steam did they resume their professional gloom.

But of all the slogans, placards and flags on view in and around Tiananmen Square, the most worrying for the leadership was surely the long red banner carried by short-haired men in uniforms. "The People's Liberation Army," it announced in large gold letters. Further along Changan, two off-duty soldiers had commandeered a Red Flag Limousine from which they waved coloured banners as they inched along towards Tiananmen. On the front bumper was strapped a piece of card with the words: "Don't ride in a Benz", mocking the Politburo's taste for imported limousines.

If even the army was on-side, those who saw them wondered, how could the students fail? The sense of imminent victory was reinforced by the realization that police had suddenly vanished from the streets around the Square. Their booths were being occupied by students. The state seemed to have abdicated all responsibility for public order, handing over control of traffic and crime to teenagers in headbands. Nor did authority now seem to speak through the official press. In its edition of May 18, *People's Daily* relegated Gorbachev's visit to a small box in the lower right-hand corner of its front page. The balance of the page was taken up by three pictures of banner-waving protesters, beneath the headlines: "More than a million people from all walks of life demonstrate" and "Save the students, save the children".

THE diversity of support for the hunger-striking students was matched by the diversity of grievances and goals voiced in their name. Some were marching for "democracy" in the conventional sense; others were more worried about inflation. Some had lost patience with the government over the rising crime rate, or because private beancurd sellers earned so much more than ordinary factory workers. The China Academy of Social Sciences spoke for those who wanted to kick out the present leadership: "Open a people's assembly and change the government now", read its placards. Its windows overlooking Changan Avenue were plastered with posters demanding that "the whole Politburo must resign ... collective responsibility, collective resignation".

Virtually all those on Tiananmen Square would, however, have agreed with the proposition formulated by Lord Acton: that power tended to corrupt and that, in the case of the Chinese Communist Party, absolute power had corrupted absolutely. The loss of respect was intensely personalized. People made a direct connection between their own general poverty and the specific wealth of the leaders and their families. This mixture of envy and contempt so overwhelmed many demonstrators that they found themselves saluting Mao Tse-tung in their chants and placards, forgetting so quickly the many terrors of that leader's long, mad dotage. It was sufficient, as one worker said, cradling a framed picture of the Great Helmsman as he marched along Changan, that "At least he wasn't corrupt". The apparent indifference of the Party to the plight of the hunger-striking students fed this strain of rage. "Your children cheat while ours starve," read one banner. "The son of Deng Xiaoping is riding in a Mercedes but the sons of the people are here."

Such personal attacks on Deng were commonplace now that the crowds had grown more confident and aggressive. "It doesn't matter if the cat is black or white so long as it resigns," ran one poster, parodying Deng's pragmatic maxim that, so long as a cat caught mice, nothing else mattered. Cartoons lampooned him as a puppeteer manipulating the Politburo or a feudal despot in imperial robes. "Xiaoping, thank you and goodbye ... Xiaoping, go back to Sichuan: your health may be good but your brain is addled ... Xiaoping, take a break."

A group of prominent academics, including Yan Jiaqi, the political scientist, put their names to what they called the "May 17 Manifesto". Far more daring than a slogan chanted in a crowd or an anonymous poster, it was a signed attack on Deng's right to rule. "The Ch'ing Dynasty died 76 years ago," it read, "but China still has an emperor without an emperor's title, a senile and fatuous autocrat ... Unless this autocrat speaks, there is no way to reject the April 26 editorial." They spoke with the confidence of victory. "The Chinese people can no longer wait for autocrats to admit their mistakes, now they can only rely on the students, on the people themselves ... The students have already used their own action to proclaim that this student movement is not turmoil but is a great patriotic movement that finally buries autocracy in China, buries rule by emperor. Down with autocracy! The autocrats can come to no good end! Overturn the April 26 editorial! Rule by old men must end! Autocrats must resign! Long live the students! Long live the people! Long live democracy! Long live Freedom!"

The mood of triumph was contagious. On Thursday, rumours swept Tiananmen that Deng had resigned. Hunger strikers clambered on top of the buses which they used as makeshift shelters against rain. They screamed deliriously and hugged one another like armistice revellers. "We've won, we've won," shouted two teenage girls from the Foreign Language Institute, clutching each other excitedly in the drizzle. "It's over."

It *was* over. But not in the way the students thought. Their protests had been tolerated, not because the Party had come to agree with them, but because it would have been even more embarrassing to have staged a bloody crackdown in Gorbachev's presence. Similarly, it had been easier to tolerate Zhao's indiscretions than to shut him up. The Soviet president had been, involuntarily, a sort of Lord of Misrule over Peking. When he left China on Thursday May 18, after a stopover in Shanghai, the harsh realities would reassert themselves.

CHAPTER TEN

Zhao at the brink

Zhao concealed the strain well. His meeting with Gorbachev had helped. The two men had seen one another as standard bearers of a new kind of communism, and laid the basis for what might have been an unprecedented era of Sino-Soviet trust. Moreover, when Gorbachev spoke publicly for the first time about China's student unrest, he had seemed to be aligning himself with Zhao's policy of conciliation. The reform of communism, he told a press conference on May 17, his last full day in Peking, was a "painful" process. But, he went on, "these are processes that we need and which, in the end, will bring us out into a new stage of development and will impart socialism with a second wind". Asked how he would have dealt with comparable protests in Red Square, Gorbachev ruled out the use of force. "We would look at them specifically and seek political methods of solving them ... on the basis of democracy and *glasnost*, so as to preserve the main values to which we have sworn allegiance."

The problem for Zhao was that Gorbachev headed the Soviet, not the Chinese, Communist Party. Even as he was giving his press conference, the Standing Committee of the Chinese Politburo was discussing the protests, and its views were moving in a very different direction. Two of its five votes were in conservative hands: those of Li Peng and Yao Yilin. On this issue, they had secured the support of a third, Qiao Shi, the opaque chief of national security. To these men, the spectacle of a million more protesters thronging the streets of Peking that day was likely to constitute a million more arguments against further hesitation.

Late that Wednesday evening, Deng Xiaoping had summoned the Standing Committee to endorse his view that the time for "political methods" was over. The time had come to call in the army. Deng, in his capacity as head of the Central Military Commission, had already ordered units across China to prepare to move on the capital. He had not called the Politburo to decide what action to take, but only to learn what he and the other veterans had decided among themselves. He expected the Politburo to serve as his rubber stamp: which it did, with only Zhao dissenting.[*] By one account, the meeting reached an angry climax. "I have the army behind me," Deng shouted. "But I have the people behind me," returned Zhao. "You have nothing."

President Yang Shangkun later recalled, in a secret speech to the Party's Central Military Commission, that Zhao "said he could not go with the line of Comrade Xiaoping and the several comrades of the Politburo Standing Committee on the nature of the student movement. So he proposed to resign, saying he could not continue." Accounts differ as to the precise timing of his offer to step down. Some say it was given after this meeting, others that it came the following morning when the Politburo resumed its discussions. In either case the Party, bound by its code of outward unity, still struggled to maintain a vestige of unity. When the late-night meeting broke up shortly before dawn on Thursday May 18, four of the five Standing Committee members visited hunger strikers in two Peking hospitals (though Yao Yilin, the oldest member, was apparently too tired by now for public relations). In front of the invited television cameras, Li Peng and Zhao both wore their best bedside manners, beaming benignly down on the students over whom they were privately warring.

That afternoon, as a million people poured into the streets for the second successive day, as Gorbachev left Shanghai for Moscow and as hunger strikers set up a second encampment outside Zhongnanhai, Li Peng lost his patience. He summoned Wuerkaixi, Wang Dan and ten other student leaders for a meeting in the Great Hall of the People. At the outset, it seemed an important concession, the first clear sign that dialogue with the leadership was underway. During Hu Yaobang's funeral at the start of the campus unrest, these same students had gathered outside the Great Hall to bellow: "Li Peng come out, Li Peng come out." Now, nearly a month later, Li Peng had still not come out,

---

[*]   Hu Qili, the fifth member, vacillated.

but had instead decided to let them in. He also let in television cameras. The entire meeting would be broadcast.

It was an agonizing experience. For perhaps the first time in his life, Li faced a group which did not know its place. They were neither fawning young officials nor venerable veterans, but a rabble of young students barely out of their teens. Even their clothing seemed to scream disrespect. While Li wore a crumpled blue Mao suit, Wuerkaixi swaggered into the Xinjiang Room of the Great Hall in a pair of striped pajamas and clutching an oxygen pillow, advertising the fact that he had just returned from hospital. Wang Dan appeared wearing a black leather jacket and a red headband scrawled with slogans. "Delighted to meet you," Li said unconvincingly. "This meeting came a little late. I apologies for this ... Even the oldest of you is about 22 or 23. My youngest child is older than you. None of my three children is involved in profiteering. Not one. They are all older than you. We look at you as if you were our own children." But the students were in no mood to be patronized. With a wave of his hand, Wuerkaixi cut the prime minister off in mid-sentence. "This meeting is not only a little late," he shouted, wagging his finger, "but too late ... it is not that you asked us to come for discussion but that the great number of people at the Square asked you to come out for a talk. The topic of discussion should be decided by us."

Had any serving Chinese leader been so addressed since, even during, the Cultural Revolution? Li Peng gritted his teeth, fingered his antimacassar and stared blankly at his grey shoes, even when one student compared the Communist Party unfavourably with the regime in South Africa. Wang Dan repeated the students' demands: full repudiation of the *People's Daily* editorial; recognition of their "illegal" organisation; and dialogue.

Eventually, the students wound down. Li then came to the real point of the meeting. He had called them in, not to listen to their views but to tell them his own. It was no longer the time, he told them, for "endless quibbling ... There is complete chaos in Peking. Moreover, the turmoil has spread throughout the country ... I can state that during the past few days, Peking has been in a state of anarchy." His pent-up emotions were hissing out like steam. He spluttered, his voice rising with barely-controlled rage. The students had lost control of the situation. "I hope that you students will think for a moment what consequences might be brought about by such a situation ... It is impossible for us to sit idly by, doing nothing. It is impossible for us not to protect the safety and lives of students, not to protect our socialist system."

THE POLITBURO Standing Committee met again on Thursday night. Again, conservatives, obeying Deng's will, planned a crackdown. Again, Zhao was isolated. He had probably slept no more than eight hours in the past three days. His composure snapped. As dawn approached on Friday morning, he made what would be his last public appearance. Shortly before five, he ordered a car to come to his office inside Zhongnanhai. Accompanied by a handful of pallid aides, he headed for Tiananmen Square. Just behind him, in a separate vehicle, was Li Peng, who, according to some accounts, had rushed from his own office to try to stop the expedition. Zhao's supporters claimed that he had wanted to visit Tiananmen Square for days, but had been prevented by his Politburo colleagues. Now, his career in tatters, he had nothing more to lose.

A few minutes later, he was climbing into a filthy, foul-smelling, laundry-bedecked bus used by the hunger-strikers as a shelter. His face drawn, his eyes puffy with exhaustion, he was a far cry from the resilient leader in business suit and striped silk tie who had met Gorbachev three days before. "I just want to say a few words to the students," he said, close to tears, through a red loud-hailer. "We have come too late. I am sorry. No matter how you have criticized us, I think you have the right to do so. I am not here to ask for your forgiveness. I just want to say that your bodies are now very weak. Your hunger strike is now in the seventh day. You cannot go on like this. We were once young, too, and we all had such a burst of energy. We also staged demonstrations and I remember the situation then. We also did not think of the consequences."

He stood in the bus for about seven minutes. Li stayed for one. After his emotional apology, Zhao lingered a few seconds longer to autograph a handkerchief, a notebook and a piece of cloth handed to him by students, then left. Back at Zhongnanhai, his offer of resignation still neither accepted nor rejected, he announced to his colleagues that he was taking three days' sick leave, and disappeared.

The appeal almost worked. Some students, sensing an imminent crackdown, urged a pullout from the Square. Zhao, they argued, was on their side. Li Peng clearly was not. By Friday afternoon, student leaders were whispering to each other about the danger of a military strike. If Zhao had not been able to tell them as much himself, his associates made sure that the message got through. That afternoon, the students' public address system in Tiananmen Square broadcast an alarming statement from four think-tanks closely linked to Zhao,[*] which employed many of the bright and bold thinkers who were trying to reform the system from within. If Zhao was finished, so were they. They resolved to warn the students just how high the stakes had become. They pleaded with them to leave the Square, saying that the leadership might otherwise "adopt strong measures such as military control ... This bleak prospect is something that the people of China, having suffered for a decade during the Cultural Revolution, cannot possibly accept."

Student leaders received other, more direct tip-offs as the day wore on. They called a series of urgent meetings to decide what to do. Their organisation, strengthened and emboldened by the success of their hunger strike in previous days, began to disintegrate under the pressure. Wuerkaixi, who had re-emerged from his earlier "disgrace," pleaded for an immediate pullout. "It was related to a very dangerous piece of news I got that night, that there was a bloody suppression coming," he would later explain. "I worried deeply about the tragedy that would surely result. I had to make the suggestion to leave or be very irresponsible." Some suggested a compromise: hunger strikers to eat but remain in the Square; provincial students to cease coming to Peking; workers to return to work. Others dissented entirely, saying that the movement had come too far to turn back.

As the students debated throughout Friday, shuttling back and forth between their "command bus" and the tents at the base of the Monument to the People's Heroes, another crowd of sympathizers and sightseers poured on to the streets. They numbered about 100,000: fewer than in the previous two days, but still a powerful show of feeling.

---

[*] The Economic Structural Reform Research Institute, the China Rural Development Research Centre, the Institute of International Studies of the China International Trust and Investment Corporation and the Peking Association of Young Economists

The students were also heartened by the impact of their example on workers. Earlier that day, a group of young workers had announced the formation of an Autonomous Union of their own. "We announce to workers across the country: the workers of Peking are getting organized," the new group said in its first tract. Unless the students' demands were met unconditionally within 24 hours, workers across Peking would stage a one-day general strike.

Li Peng was unimpressed. At two o'clock that afternoon, he met Richard Woolcott, an Australian foreign ministry official, at Zhongnanhai. For forty minutes, they clove to the intended topic of economic co-operation. Then, agitated and increasingly impatient, Li suddenly diverted the conversation. How did his guest arrive at Zhongnanhai? The Australians, who had picked their way along side-streets, sensed a trap — an attempt to secure, for publicity purposes, foreign confirmation that Peking was in "turmoil". They replied that they had taken a different route, but that the journey had been all the more interesting as a result. Li snorted. Foreigners, he said, should "not have to take side-streets". He finished with a warning. "Turmoil has broken out in Peking," he told Woolcott. "The Chinese government will take steps to stop it." The declaration was meant for public consumption. By the time the Australians returned to their embassy, Li's words were already being broadcast by the Xinhua News Agency.

CHAPTER ELEVEN

Martial Law

The seven o'clock news on the evening of Friday May 19 juxtaposed Li Peng's warning with Zhao's tear-stained face. The Party was speaking with two voices, but it was clear which would prevail. As darkness fell, motorbike riders brought back sketchy reports from the outskirts of the city: the army was closing in from all sides. Student leaders huddled in the banner-bedecked bus which served as their temporary headquarters. A statement emerged: the hunger strike was off but the occupation of Tiananmen would continue. "We have won a great victory because the people support us ... We will end our fast and adopt new methods to protect democracy."

As the news was being broadcast, high army and Party officials were gathering for a meeting of their own, in the assembly hall of the army's General Logistics Department, a walled compound off Wanshou Road in the far west of the city. The first officials began to arrive around six o'clock. Many were delayed: some by traffic jams, others by more delicate political considerations. One of the last to arrive was Hu Qili, the Politburo Standing Committee's floating voter. He finally turned up just as the meeting was due to begin, to take his seat on a raised platform reserved for top Party and state leaders. Alongside him were three other Standing Committee members, Yao Yilin, Qiao Shi and Li Peng, as well as President Yang Shangkun and Vice-President Wang Zhen. Before them sat row after row of ageing officials and military officers in uniform.

One man was conspicuously absent. Zhao Ziyang had sent word at the very last minute that he was "ill". Though it was no secret that he disagreed with the policy about to be enunciated, his rivals whispered that Party discipline was being flouted. He should be there to project an image of unity for the television cameras. As Yang would later complain with more than a touch of understatement: "The people could immediately spot that there was a problem."

Shortly after midnight, the dozens of loudspeakers attached to lamp-posts around Tiananmen Square spluttered into life. The proceedings of the meeting were being broadcast on radio and television, and the authorities were keen that the students should not miss them. The first, high-pitched voice was immediately recognizable as that of Li Peng. "The anarchic state is going from bad to worse," it squealed. "Law and discipline have been seriously undermined ... A handful of people are using the hunger strikers as hostages to coerce and force the Party and the government to yield to their political demands. They have not an iota of humanity." The television images were even more alarming than the words. Li wore a black Mao suit and thrust his fist robotically in the air while the audience applauded obediently on cue. "The fate and future of the People's Republic of China, built by many revolutionary martyrs with their blood, faces a serious threat ... A very promising China with a very bright future would become a hopeless China." Deng's treasured editorial of April 26 was back with a vengeance. But this time, Li explained, there would be more than just words. "Under such circumstances, the Communist Party of China, as a ruling party, and the government responsible to the people, are forced to take resolute and decisive measures to put an end to the turmoil."

After another wave of applause, a second, deeper voice began to echo around the Square. It belonged to Yang Shangkun. "To restore normal order and to stabilize the situation, there is no choice but to move a contingent of the People's Liberation Army to the vicinity of Peking ... If this state of affairs is allowed to continue, then our capital will not be a capital." The television cameras panned across the room to show uniformed generals clapping dutifully in support. "There was no other choice ... But I would like to explain that the troops' arrival is definitely not aimed at dealing with the students."

The students were not convinced. As the initial shock faded and the loudspeakers began to repeat the speeches, the Square erupted. Students jeered, workers chanted their support and a cavalcade of motor vehicles raced up and down before the Forbidden City, horns blaring and passengers screaming. The chorus of the *Internationale* passed from group to group of students huddled in buses or sitting on the ground. "Down with Li Peng, down with Li Peng ... down with military rule ... long live the people." The students turned up their own public address system to maximum volume. They declared that the hunger strike would be not only resumed but expanded to embrace everyone on the Square. Convinced that the army would arrive any minute, thousands of students poured out to the perimeter of Tiananmen, joining hands to form a giant human chain. "We came on our feet," screamed a banner hoisted on to the Monument to the People's Heroes, "we will leave on our backs."

Ironically, while Tiananmen Square was receiving alarming reports of troops moving into Peking, the General Logistics Department was receiving more immediate and — from its own perspective — no less alarming reports: the troops had stopped moving. All around the city, tens of thousands of people had flooded into the streets to bar entry to the capital. To the south, on the main highway leading to Peking, more than a hundred trucks filled with soldiers had been enveloped by crowds and forced to stop their advance. To the north, another column had been halted near the Summer Palace. To the east, a dozen tanks had been surrounded by peasants near the village of Tongxian. And, perhaps most galling of all for President Yang, only a few hundred yards from where he and other officials were meeting, another force had come to a grinding halt near the People's Liberation Army's general hospital.

The people's army had been outmanoeuvred by the people. Without orders to open fire, troops sat disconsolately in the back of canvas-covered trucks, cradling their AK-47 rifles. Around them swarmed not only students in headbands but workers, old women, middle-aged cadres, all of them chanting "go home" and "the people's army should love the people". At the Jing Yuan crossroads near the Military Museum, there were even patients dressed in striped pyjamas from a nearby hospital. At every cluster of stalled military trucks, students lectured the troops through loud hailers on the democracy movement and bombarded them with Maoist rhetoric. "The army is the army of the people's own sons and brothers; how can you attack your own family?" screamed one student from atop a bus wheeled out to form a barricade in the eastern district of Chaoyang. The crowd, intoxicated with "people power", flashed victory signs and cheered. "Even if they open fire, for every person they kill, ten more will rise up." The soldiers looked on blankly. They had been ordered to Peking not to do battle, many assured the students, but for "an exercise".

ANGER and confusion gripped the military. Originally, it had planned to declare Martial Law on May 21. But desperate to seize the initiative, it brought forward the order. At half-past nine on the morning of Saturday May 20, Radio Peking announced that Li Peng, as prime minister, had signed the declaration. Martial Law would take effect half an hour later.

At 10.30, the loudspeakers on Tiananmen Square thundered into life. From the government's broadcasting centre in the Great Hall of the People they boomed out Martial Law Order Number One. It said that Martial Law was being imposed in eight districts of the capital; processions, demonstrations, boycotts and strikes were banned; no one was allowed to spread rumours; the constitutional right of assembly was formally taken away; speeches were forbidden; no one was allowed to hand out leaflets or draw up petitions. The security forces and the army were authorized to adopt "any means to handle matters forcefully". Two more decrees followed. All journalists, Chinese and foreign, were forbidden from reporting or filming in the Martial Law area without official approval. Foreigners were banned from "getting involved" in any activities by Chinese citizens which violated Martial Law. It was, in effect, a blanket ban on press coverage.

Foreboding swept the 100,000 protesters who had stayed on and around Tiananmen Square overnight. The soldiers had been stopped in the suburbs, but for how long? Expecting them to break through into central Peking at any moment, students prepared for the unknown: at best, an orderly dispersal; at worst a savage attack. Tearfully, they asked strangers to take a group photograph, or passed round t-shirts for others to sign. The more thoughtful were dipping scarves and handkerchieves into buckets of water, as a precaution against tear-gas.

Throughout the day, helicopters buzzed the skies overhead, causing a brief panic below as they swooped to drop missiles. These turned out to be nothing more lethal than pamphlets supporting Li Peng. The student loudspeakers fought to drown out the Martial Law propaganda from the authorities' rival system. "Keep calm," howled the student system, "Obey orders only from this broadcast station." Signs of paranoia were evident. A warning was broadcast against stepping on pavement gratings, for fear that they might be electrified. The subway system had closed down just as Martial Law was announced, triggering fears that it had been commandeered by the army.

The students believed the soldiers would prefer to advance on them that night, just as they had attempted to do the previous evening. Blockades were set up along Changan at five-hundred-yard intervals. As dusk fell, anxiety intensified. Throughout the night, few, if any, slept. The packs of Peking youths with motor-bikes, who called themselves the "Tiger Brigades," roared around the city checking on the movements of the security forces, and reporting back to the Square. The student loudspeakers broadcast one rumour that the troops would advance two o'clock in the morning; another that they would come at four. But by three o'clock, the students sensed that they were safe for at least this one night. In recognition of victory, the loudspeakers played Beethoven's "Ode to Joy."

As dawn broke, spirits had risen to the point at which the bravest could convince themselves that Martial Law was yet another facade erected to conceal the leadership's paralysis. "The whole people have stood up," said a workers' union leader on Tiananmen, echoing Mao, "the Government has become a tiny handful." And, in a sense, the claim was literally correct. The conventional machinery of government *had* ceased to function in Peking. From the point at which Martial Law was declared, authority rested solely with a body which called itself the Martial Law Enforcement Headquarters. It had no published address, and no identifiable membership. On Sunday, it spoke for the first time. Its tone was not encouraging.

The troops, it acknowledged, had been "somewhat blocked" in their attempts to enter Peking. They were "awaiting orders." They would "firmly carry out the orders of the government...and they have the duty to adopt *every* effective measure to put an end to the situation." A new wave of anxiety, this time close to panic swept the Square — doubly frightening, because the students now knew that, despite the blockades, the army was finding its way into the city. Less than a mile from the Square, a 13-carriage train pulled into Peking's main railway station, loaded with about 2,000 armed soldiers. A column of 300 students immediately set off by bicycle for the station, blocking the main entrance. Others swarmed on to the tracks. "Cowards, come down and talk," those left on the Square howled towards the Great Hall of the People. Propaganda brigades ran out into the nearby streets, crying for support from residents and passers-by. A traffic sign pointing the way to Tiananmen was plastered with messages: "Forty years ago, the People's Liberation Army entered Peking, our fathers rushed into the streets to welcome it. Today, forty years on, the People's Liberation Army is again entering Peking, but the people are opposing it. Such is the difference between winning and losing the hearts of the masses."

As dusk fell, the soldiers were still sitting in their train carriages, cleaning their guns and biding their time. The students feared, as they had done on Saturday, an attack by night. Their own loudspeakers were now relaying a purported "ultimatum" from Li Peng, that if the Square was not evacuated by five in the morning, it would be cleared by force; hospitals had been emptied to receive for casualties; cleaning staff had been rostered for the early morning to mop up the blood. Students vowed to stay, and prepared, once again, for the worst.

Whatever the origins of this rumour, it provoked a response from the army. Late that night, television programmes were interrupted to make way for an enigmatic announcement issued in the name of the army's two most venerable figures, Marshal Nie Rongzhen, 90, and Marshal Xu Xianquan, 87. They were said to have denied "groundless rumours" that the student movement was about to be suppressed; that Li Peng had categorized the movement as a "rebellion"; and that the emergency services were standing by. The troops, they said, were moving into Peking under Martial Law solely to safeguard social order and stability. They asked the students to leave the Square for the sake of national prestige. But under no circumstances, said Marshall Xu, was the army willing to see a bloody incident. On the contrary. It would do anything to avert it.

Some students suspected a trick; others slept a little easier that night. The next day, Monday May 22, brought a still more extraordinary declaration. Seven retired military officials of the highest ranks, including a former defence minister, Zhang Aiping; a former chief of staff, Yang Dezhi; a former navy chief, Ye Fei; and the former director of the Academy of Military Science, Song Shilun, petitioned the authorities to end Martial Law. "To keep the situation from worsening," they said, "the army must not enter Peking."

The petition was sent as a letter to *People's Daily*. Though it was never published, copies found their way on to lampposts all over the city. It was unarguably intended as a vote of no confidence in the prime minister, Li Peng, the man who had signed the Martial Law decree.

Li's opponents were making a last-minute effort to discredit him. Central to their hopes were the powers of the Standing Committee of the National People's Congress, which could in theory both call a prime minister to account and abrogate Martial Law. One of Zhao's allies within the NPC Standing Committee, Hu Jiwei, was canvassing signatures to convene an emergency session for just these purposes, in the expectation that Zhao would be able to count on the support of Wan Li, the NPC Chairman. Wan had been in North America when Martial Law was declared. He had praised the students as "patriots", and urged restraint, saying that China's problems could only be settled through democracy and the legal system. Zhao's office promptly sent a telegram to Wan asking him to return. Li Peng sent another, telling him to stay. Wan decided to cut short his visit.

As the guerilla war between supporters of Zhao and Li Peng raged within Zhongnanhai, rearguard actions were fought in the coded pages of the Party press. Hu Qili, the Politburo member in charge of propaganda, counted as a fair-weather friend of Zhao; so, too, did Rui Xingwen, head of the Party Propaganda Department. Li Peng by-passed them by setting up a five-member "Press Guidance Group" of hardline loyalists, with Yuan Mu as its most visible spokesman. The two camps fought for column-inches in each issue of the *People's Daily*. The left-hand side of the front page might carry a gritty statement from the Martial Law authorities ordering obedience and praising the soldiers, and, below, messages of support for Li Peng from the provinces. The right-hand side — the symbolism was not over-subtle — would tell a different story: the people of Peking had stopped the army from entering the city because they feared bloodshed.

In Shanghai, a newspaper printed a photograph of Winston Churchill giving a "V" sign, the student symbol, amid columns of official announcements on Martial Law. Even the Xinhua News Agency nodded. On Tuesday May 23, when the students held their first big march under Martial Law, Xinhua said one million people had turned out. This was an enormous exaggeration, noted by all who had taken part — the figure was closer to 100,000 — and broke with Xinhua's tradition of understating such crowds. "The overwhelming majority of the slogans of the parade," Xinhua went on to say, "were directed against the chief leader of the State Council".* Television, in an early-morning programme for English-language students, offered a new item of vocabulary which also seemed aimed, none too obliquely, at the nation's leadership and the people's hopes: "Dinosaurs, extinct."

The lines of tanks, armour and lorries, halted along suburban streets and country roads by crowds sitting or standing in their path, had made an awe-inspiring sight over the weekend. On Monday night, tensions rose briefly near Fengtai, a village on the southwestern edge of the city, where one of the biggest of the columns — 72 armoured vehicles and 300 lorries — was waiting. It attempted to move forward. When police and troops used wooden clubs to clear a path, protesters replied with stones. But the alarm soon subsided. The troops were not advancing into Peking, but withdrawing into a base a few hundred yards away. Around the city, other columns were retreating from view. The stale-mate had been broken. Whatever the army was planning, the students now seemed safe from a *blitzkrieg*.

In the city, the tension eased to the point at which, around Tiananmen, it was as if the Party had blessed a *de facto* People's Commune of Peking. The citizens controlled the streets; the police melted away, or joined the cause. The alleys buzzed with the sound of people talking openly, able to argue about politics without looking over their shoul-ders. Students in headbands directed traffic, organized water and food deliveries and maintained order so successfully that they claimed crime had fallen. On the Square itself, they ran a bureaucracy-in-miniature with a system of security clearances and passes to restrict access to the "command centre" at the foot of the Monument to the People's Heroes. For each one who grew tired, another was arriving from the provinces at Peking railway station, bringing news of sympathy demonstrations and strikes throughout China.

On Tuesday, Peking was regaining a semblance of normality. Public utilities began working again; barricades came down; shops were reopening, and businesses were returning to work. But it was an illusory interlude. That afternoon, as if to dramatize in a single gesture the

---

*   Li Peng.

traumas wreaked by the students upon China's established order, three men from Hunan, Mao's own province, threw eggshells filled with ink and paint at the Great Helmsman's giant, iconic portrait hanging over Tiananmen Gate. They were grabbed by students, who said they were *agents provocateurs*, and handed over to police.[*] Whatever the truth, the "sacrilege" against Mao was followed by an act of God which the students, for all their intellectual rationalism, saw as a portent of momentous change. A dust storm and torrential rain swept Peking. A clear blue sky suddenly filled with dark clouds and fierce winds whipped across Tiananmen Square. It was, the students said, a clear sign that the "mandate of heaven" had slipped: but it would be a few days yet before they realised in whose favour.

HU Jiwei's plan to bolster Zhao, through the intercession of Wan Li, failed. The plane bringing Wan back from the United States went not to Peking, but to Shanghai. There, he was met on Thursday May 25 by Jiang Zemin, the city's Party boss and a well-connected ally of the hardliners in Peking. Jiang persuaded Wan, a long-time bridge partner of Deng, that it would be better for him to stay put in Shanghai. Wan agreed, for "health reasons." His illness, however, seemed to be political in nature: he was not admitted to hospital, but was confined to an official Guest House near the airport.

Zhao could now claim few public supporters, and almost none of real importance. By Thursday, six of the seven national military regions, and 27 of the 29 provinces, had made declarations of open support for Martial Law. The Army High Command commended the troops around Peking for their efforts, and repeated Li Peng's accusation that a "small group" was responsible for creating the chaos. The State Council ordered provincial governments to stop students leaving for the capital.

Finally that Thursday night, Li Peng emerged. He was seen on television greeting newly-accredited ambassadors from Burma, Mexico and Liberia. He told them that his government was stable and capable. Martial law had been misunderstood. It had been declared to

---

[*]   They were later sentenced to life imprisonment for "counter-revolutionary incitement".

safeguard stability and the people's interests. The troops had met with "some obstructions," and so had not entered the city centre. "People with common sense," he said, "can all see that it is *not* because the PLA units did not have the capability to enter the city, but because our government is a government of the people and our army is the people's army. Because the people still do not fully understand the meaning of Martial Law, the army has acted with utmost restraint to avoid conflicts."

The reaction gathered pace. On Friday, the Party's Central Advisory Commission met in emergency session. Its members, Long March veterans and conservative Marxists, delivered their crusty verdict. "We must never make concessions," said the 84-year-old chairman, Chen Yun. "Not only is there the danger of losing the achievements of 10 years of reform, but there is also the danger of losing all the fruits of revolution and all the achievements of socialist construction." Then, in perhaps the worst piece of news for the students so far, the Peking military region, the only one still to have remained silent on Martial Law, declared its support. Its Party committee explained that it had been preoccupied with "seriously studying" speeches by Li Peng and Yang Shangkun, and that it was now ready to "obey orders in all action."

On Saturday, a week to the day after Martial Law had been declared, Wan Li announced that he was no longer "unwell". He was also no longer an ally of Zhao. In a "written speech" from Shanghai, he explained that he had now had time to study the situation.* The students should not look to the National People's Congress to debate Martial Law, nor to challenge a prime minister. That was the Party's prerogative. The protest movement had been hijacked by an "extremely, extremely small number of people" who were deliberately using it to create turmoil, to overthrow the leadership of the Communist Party and change the socialist system. The students' "legitimate" demands could only be addressed in conditions of stability and unity, he added.

It was left to another veteran, Li Xiannian, Yang's predecessor as state president, to deliver the *coup de grâce* to the students' hopes in a

---

*   The speech was not "written" so much as "rewritten". The original draft had been sent to him from Peking.

televised speech that same day. For the first time in public, the finger of blame was pointed on high. "One important cause of the current complex situation," said Li Xiannian, "lies with a few individuals within the leading strata of our Communist Party." The phrase left no doubt that the hardliners wanted Zhao sacked and disgraced. They still, however, needed the Central Committee to fall into line. Many of its 175 members, called to Peking to prepare a meeting that would formally dismiss Zhao, still hesitated.

That weekend, on walls and lampposts around Peking, appeared copies of a secret speech made the preceding Wednesday by Yang Shangkun to an expanded meeting of the Central Military Commission. It gave a detailed account of the conflict within the leadership, and confirmed that Zhao had offered his resignation. Peking, Yang said, was out of control. There was trouble in almost every province and city. It would lead eventually to the overthrow of the Party and the government. "We can no longer retreat. We must launch an offensive," he declared.

But first, Yang said, the Party had to be sure that the soldiers were "convinced" of the need to put down the rebellion. There was, he said, "No problem among the comrades at major military region level," but he was more cautious about "officers and men at and below the army corps level." [*] Rather than risk mutiny, the army would take its time. When troops arrived at their forward base, they would "settle down and take a good rest". Only then would they be mobilized.

This, not "people power," had been the explanation for the troops' retrenchment around Peking that week. The commanders wanted to be sure that, when the time came, their soldiers would do the things which were asked of them. If they declined, concluded Yang, then the army had a solution to that, too. It would punish them "according to military law." In China, that meant a bullet in the neck.

---

[*]   Resistance was particularly strong in the two most professional, least politicized branches of the People's Liberation Army: its air-force and navy units. Six weeks after the crackdown, their loyalty was still being challenged. "Many people (in the air force) have yet to gain a clear understanding of the roots and inevitability of the turmoil, and many ideological questions have yet to be resolved," said Radio Peking. It was also noticeable that China's defence minister, Qin Jiwei, was by-passed during the imposition of Martial Law.

CHAPTER TWELVE

A fading flame

By now, the last days of May, Tiananmen Square was filthy. The latrines near the Museum of Revolutionary History, holes in the ground surrounded by grey canvas tarpaulins, reeked of urine. The banners hung limply from bamboo poles, or snarled themselves around lampposts. Old shoes, ripped jackets, plastic wrapping, empty food packets and trampled leaflets covered the paved ground between the tents and shelters. The students had presented the Communist Party with its most dramatic spectacle of public defiance in 40 years of totalitarian rule. But they were tired.

The elite from Peking's universities had ceded their places to less disciplined newcomers from the provinces, who, undermined by fatigue, frustration and squalid conditions, were branding one another as "opportunists" and "government spies." Rows broke out over access to the public address system. Complaints were rife that the "commanders" were allotting themselves better tents, food and equipment. Some were suspected of pocketing thousands of pounds donated by sympathizers in Hong Kong and the United States.

"The major issues were no longer dialogue, recognition of the union or even the editorial," recalled Wuerkaixi, "the major disagreements were over whether to retreat or not." He and Wang Dan made their last joint appearance at Tiananmen on May 27. They announced the "final" rally for May 30, after which the Square would be abandoned. They promised that the movement would continue in a "new form," and spoke of using their universities as centres for a free press and free speech. Chai Ling was asked by an American television reporter what would happen next. "Bloodshed," she replied, "That is what I want to tell them. Only when the Square is washed in our blood will the people of the whole country wake up." But she kept her forebodings to herself.

"How can I say such things. The students are so young. I feel responsible for them. And I feel that I too must continue to live to fight for the revolution."

Chai Ling helped bring her nightmare closer to reality. At the May 27 meeting, she first joined Wuerkaixi and Wang Dan in their decision to leave Tiananmen, and began sounding out foreign friends who might help her flee the country. But then, when an orderly departure proved unpopular with the provincial students, she changed sides, agreed that they should stay after all, and placed herself at their head. A new leadership, shorn of Wuerkaixi and Wang Dan, called a new "democracy march" the following day, which attracted about 50,000 — a far cry from the million for which its organizers had hoped. The "stayers" looked ahead to June 20, when the Standing Committee of the National People's Congress was next due to meet. In the meantime, they had one last trump card to play.

On Tuesday May 30, the students presented Peking with their "Goddess," a 30-foot-tall white plaster statue of a caucasian-featured woman holding a flaming torch in both hands. Though it was called the "Goddess of Democracy," the resemblance to the Statue of Liberty was more than coincidental. It arrived during the night in three parts, on flat-bed pedicabs, from the Central Institute of Fine Arts, and was erected on the northern edge of Tiananmen Square, staring across — as Hu's and Gorbachev's images had once done — at the portrait of Mao Tse-tung hanging over the entrance to the Forbidden City. The unveiling was marked by firecrackers, speeches, and banners carrying the by-now routine demand for Li Peng's resignation.

The Goddess was, in every sense, an alien monument. The Party would later cite it as evidence that the "counter-revolutionary rebellion" at Tiananmen derived its inspiration from the United States. "This is China, not America," snarled an outraged "intellectual" quoted by state television, "Even if it were, you would not be allowed to put up a statue in front of Congress without the permission of the authorities." Most media baulked even at calling the statue by its intended name, but referred to "The Goddess of Something-or-other". Petty legal challenges were used to attack it without directly acknowledging the insult which it represented. City authorities dusted off a 1981 by-law banning structures on Tiananmen; they also claimed that the Goddess was blocking the spot where a portrait of Sun Yat Sen, the founder of China's Republican movement, was hung on national holidays.

The people of Peking were bemused by the surreal apparition, and by the students' cheek. A hundred thousand had gathered at Tiananmen in anticipation of its arrival. Thousands came in succeeding days to stare. The statue stared back over their heads, brandishing its white-plaster torch of democracy towards Mao. The symbolism would have been grossly offensive at the best of times. Now, with the Communist Party already enraged, it was an almost suicidal provocation. A day later, the Martial Law Enforcement Headquarters announced that troops in plain clothes had moved to take control of ten "key points" of the capital, including the railway station, airport and telegraph office. "They are now starting to put on their uniforms," it said menacingly.

"SMASH the traitors to smithereens," cried one poster. Another showed a giant black hammer, about to crush the "People's Enemies." Peasants waved coloured pennants, on which were emblazoned such slogans as "Oppose turmoil", and "Resolutely uphold Li Peng's important speech". The government had belatedly decided to counter the student demonstrations by staging one of its own. On May 31, it bused 4,000 people, most of them school children and farm labourers, to a football stadium in Daxing County, south of Peking. The event was officially described as a "spontaneous display of anger against bad elements". Most of the audience sat giggling on the grass, while officials thrust their fists into the air and chanted slogans from the stands. The climax came with the burning in effigy of Fang Lizhi, and an unnamed "conspirator" whom those in the know presumed to be Zhao Ziyang.

More such "anti-chaos rallies" were planned for villages around the capital, to the enormous amusement of those who could be found to attend. In the city centre, Party propagandists ordained that long red banners should be hung from public buildings. Luxury hotels were particularly popular locations. Foreign tourists, had they been able to read Chinese characters, would have been invited to share sentiments including "Long Live the great, glorious and correct Communist Party of China," and "Resolutely oppose bourgeois liberalisation." They would probably have wondered what all the fuss was about.

Gawkers at the Goddess apart, the students were losing their grip on the popular imagination. Fewer than 5,000 were now camped on the Square, sleeping on groundsheets or padded cotton jackets beneath their makeshift shelters, oblivious to the photographers moved methodically amongst them, amassing the portraits which would take their place in the records of the police and public security forces. On Friday June 2, they tried to recapture past magic with a second hunger strike. History repeated itself as farce. It attracted four people, three of whom were prepared to fast for just three days. The fourth, Hou Dejian, a popular songwriter who had defected from Taiwan, said he could go hungry for no more than two days. He would be cutting a new record in Hong Kong the following week, and could not risk his health.

The quartet began melodramatically on the terrace of the Monument, unfurling a huge white banner bearing the words, "No other way." The political scientist, Yan Jiaqi, came to give encouragement. "In the circumstances, there is nothing else we can do," he said. Others felt differently. No crowds poured into the Square to support this strike. Even the Peking Municipal Party Committee, not noted for its levity, thought it safe to scoff. It called the event a "two-bit so-called hunger strike".

Night fell.

Memorial tributes to Hu Yaobang, on the Monument to the People's Heroes in Tiananmen Square. This was the genesis of the protest movement.

Above: Mikhail Gorbachev, the Soviet leader, received at Peking airport by President Yang Shang-kun (Xinhua); Right, top: Zhao Ziyang, Communist Party general secretary, addressing hunger strikers in Tiananmen Square at dawn on May 19 (Sygma); Right, bottom: Qiao Shi, of the Politburo Standing Committee, visiting hunger-strikers in hospital. (Sygma)

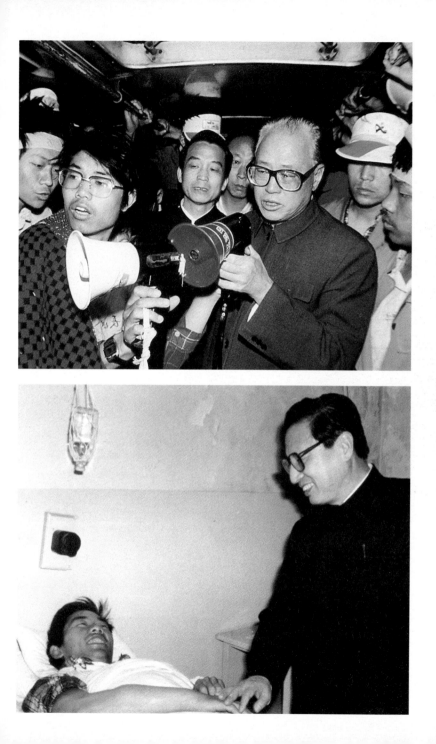

May 20 on Tiananmen Square. Protesters settle down for the night. In the centre rises
the Monument to the People's Heroes, with Chairman Mao's Mausoleum beyond. (Fred Scott)

Chai Ling (left), Wuerkaixi (centre) and Wang Dan (right) address students on Tiananmen Square. The three would later head the government's list of "most-wanted" student leaders. (Durand/Sygma)

Three faces of the "turmoil": Deng Xiaoping (top); the portrait of Mao Tse-tung on Tiananmen Gate, defaced by vandals (below, left); and Li Peng, the prime minister.   (Xinhua, Reuter, AP)

The "Goddess of Democracy", under construction in the Central Institute of Fine Arts, Peking. It was transported in three sections to Tiananmen Square on the night of May 29.

The final gesture of defiance: the "Godess of Democracy" stares out across Tiananmen, now under Martial Law, on May 30. Five days later, it would be crushed by the advancing tanks.

The view westward into Tiananmen Square after the June 4 assault, with the tanks of the People's Liberation Army in occupation. (Fred Scott)

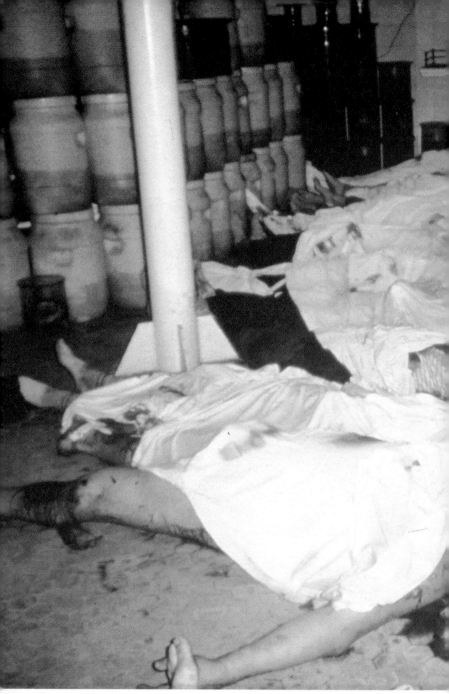

The mortuary of a Peking hospital on June 6. About 4-500 civilians were brought, dead or dying, to hospitals and clinics in the city over the weekend. (Langevin/Sygma)

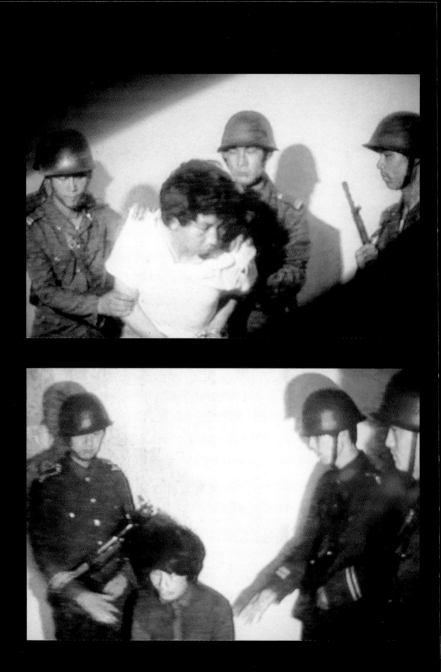

Scenes from the televised interrogation of "counter-revolutionaries". After the massacre, government propaganda depicted soldiers as heroes, and protesters as criminals. (Fred Scott)

CHAPTER THIRTEEN

Friday-Saturday, June 2-3

The first ripples of the advancing storm touched Peking late on Friday night. A jeep from an armed police unit on loan to the state-owned Central Television killed three people. It overturned near the Muxidi intersection, two miles west of Tiananmen along Changan, as it sped into the city. Even before the ambulances had arrived, news of the crash had reached Tiananmen. It was not an ordinary traffic accident, the student loudspeakers blared, but the advance guard of the long-awaited assault. Several hundred students sped off on bicycles west towards Muxidi. From the east, soon after midnight, came more alarming news. Soldiers were advancing. For the first time since troops had come to Peking two weeks before, it was not a false alarm.

With the barricades down and the students' guard lowered, there was nothing to stop them. Jogging in a tight column, about 5,000 unarmed young soldiers appeared as if from nowhere, heading in along Changan towards the Square. A mile from Tiananmen, they ran into their first opposition, traffic dividers pulled across the road as makeshift barriers. It did not stop them. They ran on, reaching the Peking Hotel within sight of the Square. The students started banging drums and broadcasting shrill appeals for help: "They're coming, they're coming." They dashed towards the troops and were joined by several hundred people from nearby alleys. By previous standards, it was a small crowd. And, to everyone's amazement, the troops stopped without a struggle. They had run 12 miles from Tongxian, a village on the eastern edge of Peking, and were exhausted, their green baggy trousers and white shirts drenched in sweat. They simply gave up. At the side of the Peking Hotel, on Chenguang Street, another column of hapless teenage soldiers was also stopped.

Students rejoiced in near-disbelief at the ease of their victory over what they took to be the army's best effort. The crowd outside the hotel, now several thousand strong, had cornered the troops against the walls of the China Ocean Shipping Corporation on the opposite side of the road. Some soldiers cowered ignominiously beneath a nearby billboard advertising a film about Mao's wartime heroics. "Go back, go back, the people don't need you here," students yelled at them. "We are all patriots ... We have no power. We have no guns." Bewildered and sometimes even weeping, many soldiers sank on to their haunches, staring blankly up at their lecturers. Others were pushed and shoved, their uniforms ripped, their backpacks torn open, leaving trails of ration biscuits, rice packs and water bottles. All looked tired and scared, adolescent peasant boys. Fear of the troops quickly turned to sympathy. "Look, they don't even give you real food," shouted a fat middle-aged man in pyjamas holding up a mouldy ration carton, marked with a long-passed expiry date. "They're just using you. You're on the wrong side." The officers seemed to have no idea of what to do next. They carried radios, but did not or could not use them. One asked for coins and went to a public telephone box, trying to make contact with headquarters. By dawn, nothing was left of the attack. Soldiers had broken away and wandered off into the crowd amid wild applause and shouts of "thank you, thank you, you should go home". Small groups walked aimlessly through back streets, asking directions. Others trekked eastward along the main road out of Peking, back to their camp.

A parallel fiasco took place west of Tiananmen at Liubukou intersection, near Zhongnanhai. One thousand people enveloped four buses carrying armed soldiers, and a jeep with officers. Gun muzzles stuck out from sacks, stacked in a jumble with ammunition boxes, garrotes and blankets. Officers sat stoically in the jeep while the mob abused them and tried briefly to tip their vehicle over. Youths jumped on the roofs of the buses. Here too, initial anger soon dissolved, as the civilians realized the helplessness of their captives. A few hundred yards further west, more military vehicles were blockaded in front of the Peking Telegraph Office. On top of one bus, students had erected a mock shrine in which they placed a box of ammunition, a book of Mao Tse-tung's military theory and a Communist Party manual. People laughed, taunting the soldiers with the Maoist dictum: "The army and the people are as close as fish and water." At Muxidi, still further out along Changan, another army bus was stopped and its contents — bedding, rucksacks, cartons of food and radios — displayed on its roof.

The troops on the streets were marooned. Inexplicably, units inside the Forbidden City and the Great Hall of the People did not come out to help them. By any normal reckoning, the People's Liberation Army had failed dismally. But it had achieved one aim: it had inflamed the entire city. For those in the leadership who had been arguing that military force was necessary in Peking, a justification was being created. Though the army's tactics *could* be explained away as incompetence, they presented a text-book example of the classic strategy recommended by China's most famous military philosopher, Sun Tzu. "When capable," wrote Sun, "feign incapacity; when active, inactivity. When near, make it appear that you are far away; when far away, that you are near. Offer the enemy a bait to lure him; feign disorder and strike him."

By noon on Saturday, after days of calm, Peking was again in ferment. People poured into the streets to peer at the stranded soldiers, hot and morose like animals in a cage. Many tried to cheer them up, filling up their canteens with water or offering food and cigarettes. Fathers lifted up their children to let them talk and shake hands with the troops. Others were more boisterous but hardly more threatening. Young men seized AK-47 assault rifles, and showed them off from the top of a bus. Rifles, helmets and bayonets were propped up like wigwams. As with any carnival, people took pictures — especially the Public Security Bureau. Video-tapes of youths waving guns, and soldiers besieged by mobs, provided the evidence that an armed rebellion had begun in Peking, and that weapons were being used against the People's Liberation Army.

But so far, there was no violence. There were, however, people trying to create it. Men in hard hats with wooden clubs roamed the city. "Fight the soldiers, kill the bastards," shouted one group of bare-chested workers swaggering along Changan towards Tiananmen that afternoon. People were shocked, and joined students in trying to calm them. Many suspected *agents provocateurs*. These fears were reinforced later in the day, when five lorries from the Capital Iron and Steel Company appeared in the west of the city with helmeted men on board. People stopped them near the Temple of the Moon and extracted a confession: they had been paid a 50 yuan (£8) bonus, the equivalent of a two-week wage, to come out and "help the soldiers". Another lorry of heavy-set men with clubs was halted in the east near the Jianguomen entrance to the city.

AT two o'clock on Saturday afternoon, serious violence suddenly lurched an alarming step closer when riot police launched a raid to recover the weapons and equipment seized at Liubukou. They were worried, the authorities said afterwards, that in the wrong hands the material might cause an "explosion". "The police are coming," screamed a student with a loud-hailer. Panic swept the crowd. Out of the western gate of Zhongnanhai hurtled some 200 police armed with truncheons, led by a squad firing tear-gas grenades. People fled down Changan hurling stones and abuse. The youths were thrown down from the buses, the weapons recovered by the police, and the soldiers set free. For half an hour, the two sides skirmished, and then the police withdrew.

A half-hour later, a thousand soldiers wearing steel helmets and brandishing rifles erupted from the back entrance of the Great Hall of the People. As they rushed out towards Changan, they were blocked by a bus hastily driven across the road and by a crowd of thousands from nearby streets and from Tiananmen Square. Once more, like their unarmed colleagues outside the Peking Hotel twelve hours earlier, the soldiers were swallowed up on all sides by a human barricade. They also declined to struggle, and squatted down in the hot sun.

The mood was cheerful, the chants bantering: "The student movement is not turmoil. Go home, go home." Some tried to entice the soldiers to join in singing the *Internationale*. Prompted by students who tip-toed among them, a small group of soldiers sang their own refrain, but then petered out into silence. Whatever their orders, they were unfathomable to outsiders. They waited there for four hours, beat up one man, and then retreated back inside the Great Hall. Their mission, it seemed, had been accomplished.

At six-thirty, the Martial Law Enforcement Headquarters issued an "urgent notice": "Lawless acts ... have infuriated the officers and men of our units and cannot be tolerated any more." It warned that from now on, no one should "use any pretext illegally to intercept military vehicles, impede and speak against the Liberation Army or obstruct the troops imposing Martial Law from carrying out their duty". There would be no more sitting dumbstruck on the street. Soldiers now had the "right to take *all* measures ... The organizers and troublemakers will be responsible for the consequences."

At eight o'clock, the Martial Law Enforcement Headquarters issued its final warning: "The situation in Peking has become very serious." A handful of thugs had created turmoil, it said. At the request of the "broad masses of city residents" the army would take "strong and effective measures ... There should absolutely be no softness in dealing with these thugs ... From now, all residents of Peking are advised not to walk on the streets, nor to go to Tiananmen Square. They should stay in their own houses, thus assuring the safety of lives and to avoid unnecessary losses."

The message went unheeded. Hundreds of thousands were now on the streets. But, Xinhua News Agency proclaimed at nine o'clock, the army was winning the trust of the people. "By their concrete deeds of ardently loving the capital, its people and young students, officers and soldiers have demonstrated that the PLA is forever the people's own army."

"ZHENDAN, Zhendan" — "Live fire, live fire", the crowd screamed. It was 11.35 on Saturday night. The People's Liberation Army had at last shown it would fight.

The first shots were fired at Muxidi, the site of the jeep accident, where Changan Avenue cut its broad, straight path out of central Peking from Tiananmen Square towards the Western Hills. Residents had seen columns of armour and troops roll in along Changan towards Tiananmen many times before, but only in peace and daylight, for military parades. This night, the highway became a scene of carnage. Few at first recognized the regular *put-put* of automatic gunfire. By the end of the night, none could mistake it.

The army had reached Muxidi at about half past eight in the evening, heading eastward as darkness was falling on the city. Six tanks and armoured troop-carriers led a convoy of about one hundred lorries. Most of the trucks carried troops, others carried supplies, with tankers in tow.

Across the city, other columns were also on the move. To the south, infantry and a brigade of paratroopers advanced from Nanyuan military airport. To the north, 25 lorry-loads of troops headed out from Shahe airbase along the main road from the Ming tombs. To the east came 30 vehicles from Tongxian. In all, more than 50,000 troops had been committed to the assault and they made their way in fits and starts towards the centre of Peking. It was the force at Muxidi, however, that everyone would remember, the main army for the push on Tiananmen Square. Its progress along Changan led people to rename its route "Blood Boulevard".

Unlike the peasant boys people had confronted outside the Peking Hotel less than 24 hours earlier, the troops at Muxidi had orders. Bystanders identified them as the 27th Army, which had been brought into Peking from Shijiazhuang on 19 April and was known as one of the People's Liberation Army's toughest units. [*]

The convoy came to a stop several hundred yards before the Muxidi bridge, which carried Changan across the old city moat. Ahead, on the eastern side, lay a hastily-improvised barricade. Three buses had been rolled out from the 114 Depot of Peking's Capital Bus Company nearby, to reinforce a pile of carts, furniture and scrap. Further back stood several trucks commandeered as a second line of defence. Thousands of residents had rushed from their homes and flats, massing behind and in front of the roadblock. Thousands more lined the banks of the canal. The crowd cut across age and class. Most of those at the barricade itself were young factory workers, but on the streets around them were office workers, journalists, writers and the privileged children of Communist Party officials. Just one or two hundred of the crowd were students, clustered around the flags of three universities. Some wore bandannas scrawled with the slogan "Dare to Die", the name adopted by self-styled "commando squads" which policed the demonstrations and guarded the student leaders. Even as the troops were massing at Muxidi bridge, the phrase still seemed melodramatic.

---

[*] Western military officials, however, believed it was a mixed force comprising elements of the 27th, 28th and 63rd Armies, all under the command of the Peking Military Region, and possibly other units.

Exercising what the government would later call "a high degree of restraint", the troops paused for nearly two hours at Muxidi. A no-man's-land separated the convoy from the crowds, some 5,000 in front of the barricade and many more behind. The two sides sparred, alternately advancing and retreating. Armed with riot shields and truncheons, but not guns at this stage, the soldiers were met by a barrage of stones, bricks and small chunks of concrete from broken paving supports and traffic dividers. Both sides took casualties, with blood and broken glass on the tarmac glinting in the bright lights of the convoy.

At 11.15, the army made its final unarmed assault. Using stun grenades to disorient the crowd, 2,000 soldiers rushed the barricade. Their advance was halted briefly, several times, but within 15 minutes they had reached the buses. A fresh hail of missiles deluged them, this time from behind the barricade. As they fell back, the mob set fire to the buses. Petrol tanks exploded into a wall of flame. It seemed as if the people of Peking had once again defeated as much force as the army cared to throw at them. But as these unarmed troops retreated, another force was preparing for battle. New orders had arrived. Further back in the convoy, several hundred new troops could be seen leaping down from the lorries in the smoke-filled half-light.

The army was finished with riot control. At Muxidi, it was ready for war. The Martial Law Enforcement Headquarters could wait no longer: the troops must take Tiananmen before dawn. Forming into small squads, the fresh troops, AK-47s at the ready, sprinted forward like commandos dashing up a beach. Then, at 11.35 on the night of Saturday June 3, they took aim — and fired at the barricade.

The opening volley, single shots, claimed few victims. Most were shielded by the buses. But within seconds, the troops reached and passed the barricade. Their backs to the burning buses and facing forward into the crowd, they fired at close range on to unarmed, unshielded civilians. Panic took over. Some tried to flee, others threw themselves to the ground. Until then the army was told: "Go home, go home." Now such a hope was impossible. They howled abuse: "Fascists", "Animals", "Mother-fuckers", every filthy insult they knew.

Many were hit in the back as they ran. A French journalist, Pierre Hurel, took refuge behind a tree. He saw at least 30 people fall. A young man standing next to him crumpled to the ground, his white t-shirt covered in blood. Hurel caught a glancing shot as he tried to flee, from a ricocheting bullet which scarred his back. The bravery at Muxidi as everywhere that night was extraordinary and foolhardy, as people regrouped against the soldiers, only to face fresh fusillades. It was too late. Their barricade had fallen.

THE KILLING at Muxidi was over in less than half an hour. At midnight, the tanks and troop carriers smashed their way through the burning buses. Behind, the convoy of lorries revved up to advance on Tiananmen Square. As they drove forward, the troops on board fired over the wooden tail gates. One armoured vehicle paused just beyond what was left of the barricade. The crowd swarmed over it, prised open the hatch, pulled out the crew, beat them senseless and set the vehicle on fire with burning debris. Red banners were draped over its gun-barrel: "Democracy", they said, and "Freedom".

The civilians dropped back into apartment doorways and dark *hutongs*, the narrow side-streets off the main road. "They're going to massacre us all," a woman yelled. Young men dashed ahead along Changan to help hold other roadblocks. "Avenge the dead, blood for blood." Some were pathetic obstacles, iron railings, branches of trees. Others were more substantial: buses again, any car or vehicle that was nearby, as at Fuxingmen, the next intersection, and at Xidan about a mile from the Square. The troops on foot hunted in packs, shooting at people who had fled down side streets.

Tricycles ferried the injured, many howling with pain from open wounds, into the *hutongs*, or anywhere to escape the shooting. Many headed for the nearby Fuxing Hospital, where the scene that night, as in all the hospitals of central Peking, was like an abbatoir. Scores of wounded, including some of the soldiers who had been caught and thrashed before being rescued by students, sprawled several to a bed, or lay on benches and the blood-smeared floor. Bullet wounds gaped out of heads, chests and legs. Some were already dead; others were bleeding fatally.

The hospitals could not cope. Supplies of plasma, bandages and dressings ran out. Hundreds of friends and relatives jammed entrances and roamed corridors. Inside the temporary morgues, they found bodies with faces so disfigured by bullet wounds that they were only identifiable by scars or birthmarks. At the Peking Children's Hospital, near the first battle, 40 casualties were admitted in 20 minutes. Scores more arrived thoughout the night. At Fuxing Hospital, 30 corpses, most of them youths, would be laid out in two rooms the next day. Relatives hid their grief and shut out the heavy stench of formaldehyde behind handkerchiefs.

Not all the injured came from the streets. Nor were they all ordinary workers. Soldiers in their savage firing had shot up one of the best addresses in China. For though the blocks of flats around Muxidi proclaimed no great distinction, two of them — Building Number 22 and Building Number 24 — were among the most exclusive in the city. Only the guards at the gates hinted that these were the homes of some of the most senior cadres of the Chinese Communist Party, officials who had attained at least the rank of vice-minister.

From the windows and balconies of these apartments, the high cadres and their families could watch the chaos outside on that terrible Saturday night. Some looked down to see their own children fighting shoulder-to-shoulder with the mob. There could have been no more extraordinary reflection of the alienation which had taken place in China than the spectacle of these young people, with their places at the best schools, their access to study-trips abroad, their expectations of plum jobs within government or industry, fighting to overthrow the authority on which their own privileges depended.

But the Party's crisis was more than a generation gap. The parents in Buildings 22 and 24 were also divided, as the Party at large was divided. Some argued against the Democracy Movement because they remembered the Cultural Revolution, and feared the cynical manipulation of the masses. Some supported the calls for cleaner and more open government, but thought that the students should consolidate a moral victory by returning to campus. Almost all wanted the Party to remain united, whichever course it took, because their jobs depended on it. Similar debates were taking place all over Peking: in the Party institutions, the ministries, state-run radio and television, even within the People's Liberation Army itself.

The "rebels" who fought soldiers along Changan had their supporters inside the two buildings. Throughout the night some put up posters condemning the violence and those they believed responsible for it. A slogan was pinned to the apartment door of Yuan Mu, the government spokesman, calling him "China's Chief Instigator of Turmoil" — a black comment on the Party's hard line towards the democracy movement. This was ripped away and replaced by a second: "China's Biggest Instigator of Turmoil." This, too, was removed and replaced by a third: "China's Supreme Instigator of Turmoil."

Soldiers shot indiscriminately into Buildings 22 and 24, terrorizing their inhabitants as effectively as they did those on the streets. Yu Shouhai, a senior official of the Hong Kong and Macau Office, was reported hit in his apartment on the 12th floor, when a bullet grazed his head and caused heavy bleeding. Two maids, whose rooms faced on to the road, were shot dead. The son-in-law of a cadre was shot while washing dishes in his kitchen. The daughter of a Chinese diplomat at the United Nations was wounded, bringing her mother rushing back from New York to a Peking hospital bed. On Sunday morning, the buildings were left pockmarked by the heavy gunfire, their windows shattered. On Monday and into Tuesday, long after the army had broken through the barricade at Muxidi and moved on to capture Tiananmen Square, the shooting continued, as it would do wherever else in Peking the roaming soldiers and tanks sensed defiance, or merely found people in their way.

Those who ordered the army into Peking, Deng and president Yang Shangkun, had done so not merely to disperse the mobs from the barricades, but to create a spectacle of forceful repression so shocking that it could not fail to cow anyone within the Party who had dared to sympathize with such defiance. The decision to open fire at Muxidi, in front of one of the Party's main residential compounds, was a part of that spectacle.

CHAPTER FOURTEEN

Saturday-Sunday, June 3-4

The students on Tiananmen Square had the trappings of a military force. As a commander-in-chief, Chai Ling; as a command centre, a tent. They mustered their only defensive weapon: words. While the People's Liberation Army readied for its assault at Muxidi, the commander-in-chief decided to hold a press conference. No one came, she complained later. "We issued a statement with only one demand: Down with the fraudulent government of Li Peng!" With Peking on edge, its citizens building barricades, Tiananmen Square a swirling mass of nervous excitement, it was pure folly.[*]

The symbolic, tragic gestures made by Chai Ling and her followers around the Heroes' Monument continued throughout the night. Their next move was to gather round the statue of the Goddess of Democracy and declare a "University of Democracy". Its campus was Tiananmen Square. They took an oath: "I swear to use my young life to protect Tiananmen Square. Our heads may be cut off, our blood may flow, but the People's Square must not be lost." Reality, though, began to close in on all sides. A young student rushed to the Monument waving a bloodstained jacket with a bullet-hole in the shoulder. Others brought bullet casings and reports of the advance along Changan.

---

[*]   Chai Ling's account of the final hours of the democracy movement was given in a tape-recorded message smuggled to Hong Kong.

"We had never imagined," said Wuerkaixi, "that the government could be so cruel and so barbarous." He had returned to the Square, he recalled later, at about eight o'clock on Saturday evening after meeting supporters from Hong Kong. "We heard the first news that a student from my university was hit in the head at Liubukou. There were tears in my eyes. In those one or two months I did not cry a lot. This was the first time I cried uncontrollably."[*]

At midnight, the war reached them. An armoured troop carrier roared eastward along Qianmen West Avenue towards the southern side of Tiananmen Square, smashing the iron-frame barriers that had been dragged across the road. These crumpled like matchsticks, buckled, twisted and flattened, sparks rising as iron hit iron. The vehicle's heavy-calibre machine-gun was covered by a cloth pouch: it was clearing a path, trying to frighten people. It succeeded. Everyone on the street scattered. The troop carrier swung left into Tiananmen Square, roared north up the roadway in front of the Great Hall of the People, made a tight circle in front of Tiananmen Gate and sped back westward along Changan. A second followed minutes later, taking the same path. But as it made a circle in front of Tiananmen Gate, it slowed down. Youths bombarded it with petrol-bombs. It caught fire, limped west along Changan and came to a stop near Xidan intersection. Two crew crawled out and were set upon by the crowd. One was killed, the other was rescued by students. They marched him back along Changan towards Tiananmen Square. As they passed Zhongnanhai, a dozen soldiers armed with AK-47 rifles rushed out, seized the hostage at gunpoint, and took him to safety through Xinhua Gate.

On Qianmen Avenue, 1,000 soldiers emerged from the shadows near Quanjude, Peking's biggest roast duck restaurant, after the two ar-

---

[*]   Wuerkaixi told the authors in Paris that he suffered an attack of his heart ailment, and
was hoisted on to the upper platform of the monument where he stayed until four
o'clock in the morning. "I was lying down but I joined hands with some people and
we sang the Internationale for a long time. I remember that very clearly....Then, at four
o'clock, as the sound of gunfire grew, I was still in the Square. I knew that if I did not
leave, students who were waiting for me might die. They carried me into an ambulance
and left." In it, he said, were four people with bullet wounds. Wuerkaixi refused to
say what happened afterwards, as he was being spirited out of China. Some western
witnesses say they saw him climbing into an ambulance, but put the time of this
sighting at around midnight.

118

moured troop carriers had smashed through the barriers. They rushed towards Tiananmen, bombarded all the way with stones and bottles. Unlike their colleagues in other parts of Peking, they did not shoot. Stragglers were seized by the crowd, punched, carried off into houses. "Why are you attacking the Chinese people? Why are you hurting them? We are all Chinese." Shortly after midnight, they reached the southwest corner of the Square. They stood there, rifles at the ready, ignoring insults from the crowd, their faces reflected in the eery light of tracer bullets which were now criss-crossing the sky overhead.

Around the Heroes' Monument, students prepared for a tear-gas attack. Others sat fatalistically in their tents. Their loudspeakers appealed for calm, not violence. "Many students, workers and ordinary citizens asked the student command for permission to use weapons," Chai Ling said. "We shared their rage...but since the start of the student democracy movement in April we have upheld the principle of keeping it peaceful." Workers on the Square ignored her, seizing iron bars, wooden planks and bamboo staves. Another armoured troop carrier roared into the Square from the east of the city, where it had smashed into a troop truck and also crushed a cyclist near the Friendship Hotel. As it approached along Changan, crowds dragged traffic dividers across the road in front of the Forbidden City. Remarkably, the feeble barrier worked, upending it like a seesaw. Set upon, it was soon on fire, the blaze casting a glow on the face of Mao's portrait. In a rage, people shouted for the soldiers' blood. "Kill them, kill them, they're not people, they're things."

In the south of the city, another force was advancing towards the Square. Near the Tianqiao intersection beside the Temple of Heaven, a favourite execution spot in 1949 when Mao Tse-tung's conquering army was settling its final scores, more crowds had gathered and more barricades had been built. As at Muxidi, troops again blasted their way through. Bullets smashed windows of shops and ricocheted off buildings. An eight-year-old boy asleep in his parent's restaurant was shot dead by a stray bullet. Sobbing with anger, his parents hung the bloody blanket outside. "Make them pay for this invasion," someone yelled. "Defend the capital." The soldiers pushed on. Less determined was another contingent which halted in the east near the main compound for foreign residents at Jianguomen. They sat in their trucks the entire night, the tyres of their lorries punctured.

By 1.30 in the morning the main column from Muxidi had reached Zhongnanhai, less than half a mile from Tiananmen Square. Its battles in front of Buildings 22 and 24 had been repeated at each main intersection, leaving a trail of burning hulks the length of Changan. People watched its terrible progress now from the *hutongs*, or lying low on the tiled roofs of nearby buildings. There were no more barricades between the army and Tiananmen. The only noise as it approached Zhongnanhai was the clanging of metal tracks and the roar of engines. The troops cheered as they passed Xinhua Gate, the entrance to the leadership compound. Two lines of soldiers guarding its entrance cheered back lustily. Student banners that had decorated the gate for three weeks had been ripped down and flags removed from the mouths of two ceremonial stone lions. Bedding, clothes, rice bowls and canteens were piled in a jumble in one corner.

After the leading vehicles had passed, a group of young soldiers began a ritual cleansing of Xinhua Gate, smashing the students' rice bowls and any other breakable remnants of the occupation. A lone army sanitary officer with a watering can on his back gently sprayed the steps and forecourt with disinfectant. Backwards and forwards, pumping the watering can in a regular motion, he moved with the care of a man spraying his tomatoes early on a summer Sunday morning. If his fellow countrymen were dying, a few hundred yards down the road, it was not his job to worry.

At around two o'clock, the column drew into Tiananmen, halting at the northwest corner beside the Great Hall of the People. It waited. For half an hour, official loudspeakers had been proclaiming its imminent arrival. "A serious counter-revolutionary rebellion has broken out in the capital," a metallic male voice bellowed. "The People's Liberation Army has been restrained for some days. However the counter-revolutionary rebellion must now be resolutely counter-attacked." The students loudspeakers squawked back defiantly.

People thronged the marble bridges leading into the Forbidden City, to watch the soldiers jump down from their trucks and gradually form a thick line across Changan. Tents, once the base of the Autonomous Workers Union, were on fire along the north side of the Square. Bushes on the other side of Changan, in front of the Forbidden City, also blazed. The whole city seemed to be burning. While the troops prepared for their final assault, a squad of paramilitary police armed with long wooden staves burst out from Tiananmen Gate beneath Mao's portrait and began beating the people on the marble bridges. A young man responded with a Molotov cocktail, hurled towards the portrait. It exploded in mid-air.

Some 40 minutes after they arrived, the troops were ready. Gunfire ripped into the crowd at the top of the Square along Changan. People stumbled and tripped as they fled back or deeper into Tiananmen Square. A bus careered out of the crowd towards the army lines, finally to be halted by a hail of gunfire. The soldiers pressed onward, shooting at will. Dozens died, until the People's Liberation Army had secured to its satisfaction the northern end of Tiananmen.

Behind the advancing troops, the tanks and armoured troop carriers drew up into single line, guns pointing south down towards the students' tents. Shouting above gunfire, the rumble of tank tracks and the propaganda bellowing from loudspeakers, Chai Ling made a last desperate appeal. "You are our brothers, you promised you would not use violence," she pleaded. "Where are you now?" The government loudspeakers gave no reply, only repeating the command that the "counter-revolution" must be crushed: "It will be impossible to guarantee safety for those who refuse to listen to advice. They will have to be responsible for any consequences."

At that dark moment of the night, Chai Ling said she told the several thousand students still left on the Monument a traditional story. "There was once a colony of a billion ants living on top of a hill. One day, their hill caught alight. The ants formed a giant ball and rolled down the hill. Those on the outside were burned and crushed to death, but the majority inside survived. Fellow students, we in the Square, we are the outer layer for the people. We know deep in our hearts that only with sacrifice can we save the Republic." They linked arms, and began to sing the *Internationale* and the Chinese national anthem. "I have just had my last cigarette. Tonight we are going to die," said a student in tears. With scattered gunfire on all sides of the Square, Chai Ling, from her command tent, announced over the loudspeaker system that those who wanted to stay on the Square should stay, and those who wanted to leave were free to go.

Troops surrounded them: on Changan to the north, on the steps of the Revolutionary History Museum to the east, inside the Great Hall of the People to the west and behind Mao's Mausoleum to the south. As the four hunger-strikers and the Red Cross medical teams quickly realized, an uncoordinated retreat would invite a random slaughter. Hou Dejian, 36, the Taiwanese pop singer, left the Monument for Chai Ling's tent and asked to address the students and workers. He pleaded with the crowd to give in any weapons which it had collected. Reluctantly it did so, making a small pile on the top terrace of the Heroes' Monument, where the hunger strikers had their tent. Workers handed in a machine gun and several rifles without bullets; students, wooden clubs.

Hou and a second hunger striker, Zhou Duo, a former sociology lecturer at Peking University, then told Chai Ling they wanted to try to negotiate terms for a withdrawal, and asked her to join them. She declined, saying she could not leave her "command centre". At the west side of the Monument, Hou and Zhou climbed into an ambulance. With the doctors who had first suggested negotiating, they sped to the north side of the Square to the main column of troops. A political commissar, Colonel Ji Xingguo, met them, listened to their request and went off to consult his superiors.

At four o'clock, while they waited, Tiananmen Square was suddenly plunged into darkness. The troops around the two negotiators began howling and grinding broken glass underfoot: they too were uneasy when the hundreds of street-lamps were doused. At the Monument, students were setting fire to a pile of rubbish for light. The Commissar came back and said the students could leave unmolested through the southeast corner immediately. Hou and Zhou returned to the monument and pleaded with the students to evacuate. "Blame me if you want. Just leave," said Hou. "It's too dangerous." With the Square still in darkness the students argued. Some shouted "capitulator" at Hou, others urged a retreat. Finally they took a voice vote. "We have achieved a big victory, " Hou begged them over the student loudspeakers. "We have made our point. We are not afraid to die, but we must leave. It is our duty to fight and regroup elsewhere." Many were crying. Voices were divided evenly.

At 4.30, the lights went back on. The students suddenly noticed the soldiers were closing in. From out of the Great Hall of the People emerged 200 commandos in camouflage kit and combat boots, with bayonets fixed in their rifles. From the south, the troops which had been shielded behind Mao's Mausoleum drew closer to the Monument, taking up positions in the hedgerows. Hou and Zhou sprinted north to the commissar, their hands in the air, to plead for more time. As his own troops moved forward, Colonel Ji treated them with coolness: "Your time is up. Just get them out". Over the government loudspeakers a new order boomed around Tiananmen: "It is time to clear the Square and the Martial Law Headquarters accepts the request of the students for permission to withdraw. All people in the Square should leave." Hou rushed back, yelling at the students to get out. The commandos — led by two veterans of China's disastrous war with Vietnam in February 1979, Zhao Yongming and Liu Jianjun — raced to the foot of the Monument to seize the microphones, amplifiers and printing press. They ripped out the wires, and smashed the generators. More fanned out into the Square to shoot at the loudspeakers dangling precariously from lamp posts.

The commandos hustled the students off the monument at bayonet-point, clubbing those who refused to move. At around five o'clock, the first of some 5,000 remaining students began to leave the Square. They linked hands beneath bedraggled banners of their schools. Others lingered at the north side of the obelisk until paramilitary riot police rushed at them with wooden staves, beating them bloodily. Students tripped over each other, crashed into railings protecting shrubbery in the panic to get away. The last finally filtered out. Hou, by this time weak from exhaustion and hunger, made his way across to the Red Cross medical shelter at the forecourt of the Revolutionary History Museum, which was helping the injured students. He was treated, and lifted by stretcher to hospital. Later, he went into hiding. At the southeast corner, rows of armed soldiers had opened the corridor agreed between Hou and the commissar. As the students filed from the monument, singing the *Internationale* and flourishing two-fingered victory salutes, the armour and soldiers massed on Changan at the north side of the Square began rolling in behind them. Tanks, supported on both flanks by armoured personnel carriers, moved at walking pace towards the monument. Lines of infantry advanced with them, shooting outwards as they moved down the Square, sniping at targets along its margins.

They were cheered and clapped by the troops sitting outside the Museum.[*] The advancing armour smashed everything in its path. The first to fall was the Goddess of Democracy, which, hit at the base, tumbled head-first and shattered. The shanty town of tents followed. [**]

Hou Dejian said afterwards that he was the last person to leave the Monument. By 5.30, the army had reconquered the Square. Or, as the mayor of Peking, Chen Xitong, put it: the Square had been "handed back to the people."

---

[*] Several eyewitnesses reported deaths on the fringes of the Square. Among them, Elizabeth Pisani, a Reuter correspondent, had left the Monument just before the lights went out, and waited at the east side of the Square. She was making her way north past the Museum as the armour started moving. As she made her way along the edge of the Square, a boy, in shorts and t-shirt, fell five yards ahead of her. He had been shot by a soldier on a troop carrier on the Square. Turning back, she counted 15 casualties lying on the museum forecourt, attended by the staff of a makeshift medical centre.

[**] Students claimed people inside the tents were also crushed. The army denied this. Zhang Gong, the senior political commissar of the forces that marched on Peking, said on June 6 that "officers and soldiers checked the makeshift tents one by one to see if there was anybody left. Only when they had made sure nobody had remained therein did they begin to demolish with vehicles the tents and other obstacles." Witnesses say they saw no such checks and that a small number of students probably stayed behind, though the vast majority did escape. For symbolic reasons, it would become a central claim of official propaganda that nobody was killed *on* Tiananmen Square that night.

CHAPTER FIFTEEN

Sunday-Tuesday, June 4-6

When Chai Ling and her followers had made their way, hand-in-hand, to the edge of Tiananmen Square, the dazed group split. A few hundred turned left and dispersed. Most turned right, heading west along Qianmen Avenue in the early morning light. They were neither harassed nor followed. Half a mile further on, they turned north, along Xinhua Street, and stumbled into Changan at Liubukou, just west of the main entrance to Zhongnanhai.

Gutted vehicles, remnants of the failed attempt to stop the army reaching Tiananmen six hours earlier, were still smouldering between Liubukou and the next junction, Xidan. Some residents had returned to reconstruct barricades. As the tail of the long disjointed student column swung into Changan at seven o'clock, a line of armoured troop carriers roared towards them from Tiananmen. Eleven people were caught and crushed, their bodies broken amid the wreckage of a bicycle rank on the edge of the avenue. As others turned back to help them, soldiers fired bullets and tear gas canisters. Pandemonium again broke out.

The students continued their flight northward, towards Peking University. "We walked on regardless, protecting ourselves from the tear gas with masks over our mouths," Chai Ling said. "But those who sacrificed their lives here would remain on the Avenue of Eternal Peace for ever and ever." Throughout the day, students brought back the bodies of their fallen comrades to Peking campuses. At the University of Politics and Law, the first school to march on Tiananmen on April

17, five bodies were laid out on tables in the main hall, shrouded and packed in ice. White paper flowers echoed those which had bloomed in memory of Hu Yaobang, seven very long weeks before. White and black mourning banners repeated a single theme: "China's soil has been cruelly fertilized by the blood of its youth."

In Tiananmen Square itself, no more than twenty minutes after the student column had departed, a fresh convoy arrived from the east, similar in size to the one which had formed the backbone of the overnight assault from Muxidi. It was led by an industrial earthmoving machine, which ploughed an easy path through the debris of barricades, pushing aside fresh vehicles which had been rolled across the road in the pre-dawn hours. It, too, fired on buildings and passers-by. The Peking Hotel was hit by bullets. The worst shooting came as the vehicles approached Tiananmen. Scores of people standing under a row of trees or sitting on benches were sprayed with bullets.

Gunfire echoed across Peking throughout the early morning, counterpointed by endless shouts of *"Ba-gong, ba-gong"* — "strike, strike". At around nine o'clock, a brief lull settled on Tiananmen Square. It was now an armed camp, blockaded at each entrance by lines of infantry and armoured vehicles. Helicopters flew in and out, bringing supplies and dignitaries to inspect the army's achievement. Small signs declared it to be a "Martial Law area, entrance strictly forbidden". At the northeastern approach along Changan Avenue, hundreds of troops crouched behind the concrete blocks which only hours before had been used as barricades against them. A hundred yards beyond, small groups of pedestrians and cyclists milled in front of the Peking Hotel. For over an hour, the troops glowered, but held their fire. The crowd gained in size and confidence, inching forward. At twenty minutes past ten, it crossed an invisible frontier. Without warning or explanation, the soldiers' guns exploded.

For one endless minute, the bullets poured out. The soldiers seemed to have no clear idea whether they were shooting to kill or merely to frighten. Some bullets went high, hitting the hotel balcony. Others went wide, scarring the walls of the Forbidden City. But many of the gun-barrels pointed straight down Changan and into the ranks of the advancing people.

As bodies crumpled to the ground, the crowd behind them scattered. An ambulance careered out of control past the wounded into a police box, bursting into flames. The army delivered a finale of machine gun fire from armoured troop carriers. Then, for a moment, the avenue was still: a hundred yard length of corpses, abandoned bicycles and prone, terrified survivors.

That first drama would repeat itself many times during the day. A crowd inched forward; troops opened fire; the dead were pulled away; and, after a lull, a new crowd began to form. The Martial Law Enforcement Headquarters had ordered the streets to be cleared: those who ventured out could be fired on at will. "Now the work to clear up Tiananmen Square has basically ended and the troops have on the whole taken up their positions," announced the mayor, Chen Xitong. "However, the situation is quite grim; the capital is still in crisis."

At one o'clock in the afternoon, Radio Peking's English-language service began its broadcast with an extraordinary announcement. "A most tragic event happened in the Chinese capital, Peking," the newsreader said. "Thousands of people, most of them innocent civilians, were killed by fully armed soldiers when they forced their way into Peking. Among the dead are our colleagues at Radio Peking ... The soldiers were riding on armoured vehicles and used machine guns against thousands of local residents and students who tried to block their way. When the army convoys made a breakthrough, soldiers continued to spray their bullets indiscriminately at crowds on the street. Some armoured vehicles even crushed foot soldiers who hesitated in the front of the resisting civilians. We appeal to all our listeners to join our protest for the gross violation of human rights and the most barbarous suppression of the people. Because of the abnormal situation here in Peking there is no other news we could bring you." At the end of the broadcast, the radio began playing Beethoven's Fifth Symphony. Its opening notes echoed the Morse Code rhythm — three dots and a dash — for "V," the symbol of the student protest.

There were four people in the studio that morning. Their shift had begun at 4.30, and all had cycled to work at the broadcasting centre on Changan Avenue through the appalling carnage all around. In charge of the shift was Wu Xiaoyong, son of China's vice-premier and former foreign minister, Wu Xueqian. Like his three colleagues, he was horrified by what he had seen. In the course of the day, a journalist from the station's Russian-language service was shot dead as he cycled home from work. For their actions, the entire English-language section of

Radio Peking was put "under investigation". Wu himself was ordered to make a long self-criticism.

On the other side of Peking at the office of *People's Daily*, journalists were also preparing to protest. Many had given earlier support to the students, with the result that plainclothes troops had been posted inside the newspaper's walled compound. They were obliged to work in nuances, but these were perfectly clear to regular readers — and the authorities. Boxed into the middle of the front page was a brief despatch, headlined "This night in Peking". It nodded to the Party line by quoting the military newspaper, *Liberation Army Daily*, as saying a serious counter-revolutionary rebellion had begun early on Saturday morning. It continued: "At around 22.00 hours on June 3, a series of shots rang out and the Martial Law troops entered the city. From midnight until the early morning, the Friendship Hospital, the Fuwai Hospital, the Peking Municipal Emergency Treatment Centre, the Railway Hospital, the Fuxing Hospital, the Xiehe Hospital and the Guanganmen Hospital, etc., continuously telephoned our newspaper to inform us of the injuries and fatalities of people received for treatment. As this report ends, the Martial Law troops have already stormed Tiananmen Square." The list was that of Peking's main hospitals. No mention was made of the government's claim that the victims were soldiers. The dead and injured were clearly civilians. The verb "stormed" was also provocative. For the army it had been a peaceful "mopping-up operation". *

Ordinary people were stunned by the army's savagery. They gathered in doorways and *hutongs* to assemble details of the night's violence or ventured out to set fire to the few trucks and buses not already incinerated. Messages were scrawled in blood on lampposts, or on the sides of buses which had been forced into barricades. One on the side of a bus addressed the prime minister: "Li Peng, you will never be at peace." And still more troops poured in.

---

*   Within two weeks the director of the newspaper, Qian Liren, and its editor-in-chief, Tan Wenrui, were sacked. They were replaced by Gao Di, a director of the Communist Party School, and Shao Huaze, the propaganda chief of the People's Liberation Army, where cadres were trained to be obedient servants.

To the west, on the outskirts of the city beyond Muxidi, the army suffered a débâcle. A second column, similar to the one which had passed there 12 hours earlier, came to a grinding halt in front of the wreckage of a barricade. For no apparent reason, 100 vehicles, mainly tanks and armoured troop carriers, stalled. Some said the lead vehicle stopped suddenly, and was rammed from behind; others, that the column had been ordered to halt by its commander. Matter-of-factly, groups approached it and told the soldiers: "Let us burn your vehicles if you want to live." The troops walked away, almost casually, and regrouped inside the Military Museum beside the road. As they had threatened, the people set fire to the convoy, moving methodically from vehicle to vehicle, splashing petrol as they went or stuffing rags into petrol tanks as fuses. No one stopped them. Where once there had been a convoy, soon there was a wall of flame.

By midnight, the column near Muxidi was a smouldering heap, cannibalized by peasants from out of town who were dismembering what was left of the engines and fittings. These yokels, who normally came to town to sell their farm produce or to look for work, scavenged through the wreckage. "*Germer!* (Hey mate!) do you think this will be any use?" they called to each other as they fingered engine parts, banged the steel hatches of the armoured personnel carriers and poked their faces inside.

Any possible rationale for the army's extravagant surrender at Muxidi only became apparent later in the week, when the government replaced its military offensive with one of propaganda. Day after day, television shots of the ruined convoy flashed on television "news" broadcasts: evidence of the resources and ruthless determination of the Party's opponents. The Peking authorities said that the army's losses between Saturday night and Tuesday morning amounted to more than 1,000 vehicles wrecked or damaged.

MONDAY was another day of brave defiance. Again, at the eastern end of Tiananmen Square near the Peking Hotel, the army shot at civilians for the crime of coming too close — this time, dozens of unarmed cyclists. "Animals, animals" shouted the survivors. Beneath the gate of Nananchizi Street near Tiananmen, an old woman sat wailing, screaming for vengeance: "Assassins. Dogs. You murdered my husband." The gate above was peppered with bullet holes. Raiding-parties of armoured vehicles and troop trucks patrolled up and down Changan, shooting sporadically but often murderously. Buildings and lampposts across the city were plastered with scribbled notes denouncing the army; beside some, the photographs of young men and women, shot dead in the violence.

The hero of that day, perhaps of the whole nightmarish week, was a young man carrying a jacket and a book-bag. An American television network later said it had tracked him down, and that he was Wang Weilin, 19, the son of a Peking factory worker. As a column of four tanks drove out of Tiananmen along Changan, he walked into the centre of the road. Arms outstretched, he blocked its course. Miraculously, the convoy came to a sudden halt, the tanks rocking on their suspension. When the lead tank pivoted to the right, Wang moved to block it. It swung back to the left; so did Wang. It was still once more. Then, Wang climbed on to the tank and shouted at those inside: "Go back. Turn around. Stop killing my people." Friends rushed from the side of the road to pull him off the tank. The convoy continued on its way.

Newspapers were not being delivered; the main television news was suspended; other reports were brief and oblique. Not a single word had been uttered publicly by a senior Party leader since the violence began. Rumours multiplied, and were recycled through faxed-in stories clipped from the newspapers of Hong Kong and Taiwan. It was popularly held that an attempt had been made on Li Peng's life, by a security guard whose girlfriend had been shot by the army during the assault on Tiananmen. The guard supposedly shot the premier in the hip. He did not: but the rumour remained current until Li appeared in perfect health on television later that week, hailing Martial Law troops with a raised-arm salute inside the Great Hall of the People.

The most disturbing rumours concerned the likelihood of a civil war led by rival army units. These quickened when, early on Monday morning, a large convoy of limousines and mini-buses left Zhongnan-hai heading out of the city, guarded by tanks and armoured personnel carriers. No one knew who was in the cars, or where they were going. But if, as it seemed, the leadership was evacuating Peking, what terrible conflict was it anticipating?

The "civil war" alarm stemmed mainly from confusion over which units had been involved in the Peking actions, and from signs of friction between commands. The force which "invaded" Tiananmen Square was generally believed by its victims to be the 27th Army. In fact, the Martial Law force was assembled from a wide variety of sources: as many as 18 of China's 24 field armies, and an elite paratroop force, the 15th Airborne. The only units freed from contributing troops were the strategically vital ones facing Tibet and India, the South China Sea and the Soviet border.

The proliferation of units sparked hope. As they moved around the city, rotating at night from the base camps on its outskirts, a fantasy emerged: that other armies were preparing to "punish" the 27th for its butchery. The "white knight" was usually held to be the 38th Army, which was permanently based near Peking to defend the capital.[*] Rumour held that, with the 38th poised to avenge Peking, the armoured vehicles on and near Tiananmen Square were bracing themselves for an attack. Some claimed to hear artillery fire, others to know of clashes between rival units at Nanyuan airfield. Thousands more troops were reported to be moving towards Peking by land and air.

The first concrete sign that the troops in the city might be preparing to confront an opposing force came on Monday evening. Two dozen tanks took up a "battle formation" on the Jianguomenwai overpass at about half-past seven, chasing the curious away with rounds of machine-gun fire. Their guns faced east out of the city, and along the north-south axis of the ring road. Beside the overpass, a line of 35 lorries and jeeps, and some 500 lightly armed troops from the 40th Field Army, rested beneath the guns. Beyond was a row of more soldiers. To some it looked as though their job was to prevent the 40th Field Army from escaping. During the night, street-lights were doused, and the tanks moved aside to allow a convoy of lorries from Tiananmen Square to pass through heading eastwards — another sign that battle was imminent, some surmised.

But if civil war was about to break out, this was no way to prepare for it. No army would leave its tanks parked on a bridge or overpass; nor would it leave its armour exposed in the middle of a road. These tanks were not expecting battle; there was no breakdown of military order; the army, whatever the reservations of individual generals or

---

[*]   Though the 38th, too, had taken part in the attack.

units, had united behind Deng Xiaoping. Only later would it be appreciated that not one of the tanks set on fire during the protests exploded. They carried not a single shell for their big guns. They were there to do precisely what they did: intimidate civilians. Some soldiers *did* shoot at one another on the streets — but largely in error. At night, with nerves on edge and soldiers on different sides of a street under separate command, one volley of indiscriminate gunfire from the shadows could scarcely fail to provoke another. The movement of troops and armour reflected an ordinary level of rotation and resupply. If people preferred to concentrate their anger on the 27th, all to the good: that would make it easier for the 38th, with its "clean" reputation, to police the city after other units had been withdrawn.

On Tuesday, there was more confusion and more hope. "Do not be afraid. We will not fight the people", said officers speaking through megaphones outside the Military History Museum near Muxidi. Because these men were from the 38th Army, they were cheered and applauded. "Take revenge for us against the 27th Army butchers," one man called out. "They are against President Yang Shangkun's army", another said. The crowd pressed refreshments on them. The scene was gratefully captured by government video cameras, as evidence of the welcome which the army presence was receiving from the people of Peking.[*]

The night was ominously quiet, and filled with rumour. Students, convinced that the universities were about to be occupied, fled their campuses. At Peking University, dormitories in Buildings 28 and 29 had already been evacuated. These buildings had served as campus headquarters of the protest movement. But now, the organisation had evaporated. Those who feared arrest were in hiding. Only students from out of town, with nowhere else to go, were left behind.

Nothing came. On Wednesday, the tanks at Jianguomenwai had gone. The troops and armour began moving out of Tiananmen Square. A convoy of tanks and lorries headed east out of the city, shooting long

---

[*]   One resident of Muxidi had troubled to record the registration markings of tanks which
    had patrolled the same street on Sunday and Monday, from which soldiers had sniped
    at helpless civilians. Two of these "friendly" tanks — numbers 504 and 505 — had
    been among them.

bursts into the air and raking buildings along Changan as they passed. Thousands more soldiers, many unarmed, left on foot. Some troops at the rear of the convoy were heard to shout, "Down with official corruption," a student chant; others on foot to call "Fire on the fascists" and "Crush the counter-revolutionaries". In western Peking, still more soldiers wore white armbands, and told people, "We will not open fire on you." Civilians did not know what to believe. Those who doubted that they had seen the last of the soldiers were proved right. The convoys were not a final withdrawal. The bulk of the force which had taken part in the assault on Tiananmen was giving way to fresh soldiers — armed with brooms as well as rifles — who would arrive in the two succeeding days. Even as the 27th Army was leaving to the east, other troops were arriving from the south. For 24 hours, convoys criss-crossed the city.

CHAPTER SIXTEEN

Afterwards

In the embassy-lined streets behind the Friendship Store and behind the high walls of their compounds, Peking's diplomats and other foreign residents had largely escaped the shooting. On Wednesday, the army brought it to their door.

Just before noon, the huge column which was heading away from Tiananmen passed the foreigners' residential compound at Jianguomenwai. As it did so, soldiers opened fire on the 15-storey blocks with a mix of heavy-calibre machine guns and lighter automatic weapons.[*] United States diplomats claimed that some apartments in Jianguomenwai were deliberately targeted as ones from which foreigners had been seen using binoculars to study the troop movements on Changan. Though no-one was injured, the barrage was deafening. Windows shattered. Bullets narrowly missed two American children and their nanny who were watching television.

A separate force of infantry arrived to surround the compound, their AK-47 rifles pointing through the mesh fencing. "Hey you up in the building," the soldiers yelled at some photographers on a balcony, "If we shoot you it is not our fault." The army claimed that a sniper had fired on its convoy. Troops moved into the buildings, searching apartments. After an hour and a half, they emerged. With them was a young Chinese man, whom plainclothes officers were dragging across the compound. "Let me explain," he was shouting. Who he was, no one seemed to know.

---

[*]   The same column shot up the World Trade Centre building, a mile further on, shattering 298 smoked-glass panes at a cost of £600 each.

Many residents had already left Jianguomenwai, or were making preparations to do so. By nightfall the compound was nearly empty, and the emergency evacuation of foreigners from China was in full swing. Embassies were besieged by their nationals, seeking refuge and advice. Thousands made their way to Peking airport in special convoys of vehicles flying every variety of national flag. None was stopped. Only "essential" diplomats and foreign journalists remained behind.

Ironically, just as the foreign exodus reached its peak, the streets of Peking became safe once more. On Thursday, people emerged to find troops in freshly pressed uniforms sweeping the debris from the roads and intersections, clearing away the barricades which the crowds had at last grown tired of rebuilding. Traffic police with white gloves were back at every intersection, ready even to direct non-existent traffic on roads which were still open only to tanks. Bicyclists tried to look nonchalant as they pedalled back on to the main roads, past the burned-out hulks of military vehicles and buses. They peered nervously past the rows of soldiers and tanks into Tiananmen. Today, the guns stayed silent. The soldiers' new orders appeared to be: "Smile, don't shoot." The army was trying to reclaim its former image, the friends and servants of the people. "Judge us by our action," they would tell passers-by who stopped to talk. They meant, presumably, their new-found restraint. "We are here to help you, you must understand." What of the dead? "Only the evil-doers were killed. They were harming the people." The Party line had been fixed.

The soldiers' stilted remarks provided an early glimpse of the comprehensive propaganda campaign which the Party was preparing to mount. It was determined to establish that the two essential characteristics of the violence in Peking had been the malice of those who animated the protests; and the virtue of the army which opposed them. Activists still at large would be hunted down, as befitted enemies of the people. Qiao Shi, the nation's security chief, called on all 47 million Party members to unite against the "counter-revolution." Those who did not would be expelled. Security forces throughout China were authorized to use "all methods" to restore order. Party Committees in all seven of China's military regions pledged their support. Li Peng, whose dismissal had been the theme of countless banners and countless chants, made his first public appearance since Martial Law. He was show on television, congratulating troops in the Great Hall of the People.

Public Notice 10, issued by the Peking municipal government and the Martial Law Enforcement Headquarters on Thursday, declared that "The Peking Autonomous Students Union and the Workers' Autonomous Union are illegal organizations. They must dissolve themselves immediately. The chieftains of these two organizations were the ringleaders who incited and organized the current counter-revolutionary rebellion in the capital ... They should surrender themselves to the public security authorities so as to receive lenient treatment. Those who refuse to turn themselves in shall be brought to justice according to the law and severely punished."

Within an hour, Public Notice 11 was being broadcast on Radio Peking. It listed the numbers of 17 telephone lines set up to receive tip-offs about the "criminal activities of counter-revolutionary rioters". To inform, it said, was a public duty. A week later, it would become a crime *not* to inform, and those who "harboured evil-doers" were to be punished.

On television, "news" was back on the air. Hour after hour of film footage showed crowds attacking soldiers, and military vehicles blazing. None showed soldiers attacking civilians. Gunfire was edited-out of the recordings. A few scenes of soldiers in hospital were shown again and again. Most of the injured had head bandages, or bruises on their face. Some were sitting or standing beside their beds. A few were in plaster casts. They were visited and praised by senior Party officials. When corpses were shown, they were those of two lynched soldiers on whom the government conferred the high posthumous honour of "Revolutionary Martyr".* Like the hospital wards, they appeared again and

---

* One, Liu Guogeng, was beaten to death by an enraged mob near Xidan intersection, after his jeep had been surrounded and overturned. Jumping clear, he shot and killed four people. His clothes were stripped from his body, he was disembowelled and his corpse hung from a bus. The other, Cui Guozheng, was a 20-year-old recruit, lynched on Chongwenmen pedestrian overpass near Peking railway station. His body was set on fire and left hanging for several days. Witnesses said he was shooting wildly into the crowd from the overpass, and killed a child. He was overpowered while changing a magazine.

again. If civilians had died, they had eluded the government's film cameras.

The Big Lie tripped easily off the official tongue. It embraced images, memories, motives, and even mathematics. Figures for the numbers killed and injured were chopped and changed, contradicted and dismissed with total insouciance. The true death toll would probably never be known, not least because the authorities forbade hospitals and clinics to release statistics. It was certainly higher than the figure of 200 announced by the authorities in their final report a month later; but it was almost certainly below the unofficial estimates of 2-4,000 made in the heat of the moment. Reports compiled privately from staff at hospitals and mortuaries in Peking in the days immediately after the assault on Tiananmen Square listed the number of civilian dead at 4-500. An unknown number of bodies never entered the hospitals' record books, but were taken away by friends and colleagues. The students also accused the army of burning some corpses on Tiananmen Square to conceal the civilian death toll. The army denied this.

After the first wave of fighting, the authorities said only that an unspecified number of soldiers had been injured. At six o'clock on Sunday morning, soon after Tiananmen Square had been taken, Martial Law Enforcement Headquarters said that more than 1,000 soldiers and their commanders had been injured, but made no mention of fatalities on either side. As the propaganda potential of corpses was more fully appreciated, the list of army dead began to grow. By midnight, Chen Xitong, the mayor of Peking, said rioters had killed or injured 1,000 army personnel. The next day, a letter issued jointly by the Central Committee and the State Council said that "dozens" of army fighters and armed police had died.

By Tuesday, while people were still being shot on Peking streets, Yuan Mu, the government spokesman, offered what he said were incomplete statistics "although they have been checked again and again". More than 5,000 officers and soldiers of the People's Liberation Army had been injured. Four hundred officers and men were missing, some of them presumed dead. More than 2,000 civilians, "including rioters who committed crimes and onlookers who did not know the truth", were wounded. "Close to 300" people had been killed. This last figure was not broken down, but included soldiers, "rioters deserving of punishment" and civilians killed accidentally. Yuan was very specific on one improbable point. "I have said more than once that the figures are not very exact, but one figure, based on the information gathered so far from the various colleges and universities, is relatively accurate. The number of dead students from Peking's colleges and universities is 23."

At the end of the month, a report appeared in the English-language *Peking Review* under the name of the Peking Party Committee, called "What has happened in Peking". It said that "many soldiers" were either burned or beaten to death, and described numerous incidents of soldiers under attack, though only four army deaths were identified in detail. No figure was given for the number of soldiers hurt. In the course of the "riot," it said, more than 1,000 people were wounded and more than 100 died. Some of the dead were rioters. Others, unfortunately, happened to be in the way. "Because there were numerous onlookers and students, some were knocked down by vehicles, some were caught up in crowds, and others were hit by stray bullets".

When Chen Xitong gave his definitive account of events to the National People's Congress on July 6, he gave a first official death toll for civilians: 200, of which, he said, 36 were college students. He also listed in detail incidents in which five soldiers were killed. The number of injured soldiers, armed police and security officers had jumped sharply to 6,000; so too had the number of civilian wounded, to 3,000. Never were civilian casualties allowed to exceed the military tally. "Such heavy losses are eloquent testimony to the restraint and tolerance shown by the Martial Law troops. The PLA is an army led by the Communist Party of China and serves the people wholeheartedly. They always are ruthless to the enemy, but kind to the people," Chen said.

The lie became so complex that, in seeking to support it, officials were constantly contradicting it. At first, only "troublemakers" were supposed to have been shot; then "people who had been misled" were added to the category; and then people who had "got in the way". Only a month later was it acknowledged that "innocent onlookers" and "doctors who had been carrying out duties" had been killed.

On June 16, twelve days after the Square had been occupied, General Li Zhiyun, chief political commissar of the 38th Army, briefed foreign reporters. They were particularly interested in his remarks about Tiananmen Square itself, principally because of the official insistence that — in the words of Yuan Mu — "In clearing Tiananmen Square, that is from 4.30 to 5.30 on the morning of June 4, the Martial Law Enforcement troops did not kill or injure a single student and other people by shooting or running them over." Yuan made no mention of the killing which had take place *around* the Square, or, indeed, what might have happened there before or after the clearance. His main concern was to prevent Tiananmen becoming as sacred to the protestors as it was to the Party.

General Li gave a different picture. "But still there were some thugs, they were still provocative to the troops," he said when asked about Tiananmen. "At this time, some of the soldiers in our units directed their fire into the Square and especially those troops that had wounded or dead soldiers in their units." He later denied the remark, but it confirmed eyewitness reports that soldiers on its perimeter had indeed fired into Tiananmen, and that those later moving down the Square with the tanks and armoured personnel carriers had swept its edges with gunfire.

A month later, Chen Xitong's official report on the incident admitted that a few students had refused to leave Tiananmen. They were forced out. "During the whole operation no one, including the students who refused but were forced to leave, died. Tales of 'rivers of blood' on Tiananmen Square, and the rumour-mongers themselves 'escaping from underneath piles of corpses' are sheer nonsense," he said. The Party's view seemed to be that the roads *around* Tiananmen did not count, for the purposes of its denial. Soldiers might have shot *from* the Square on to the roads, and from the roads into the Square. People might have died: but not one died standing on the sacred stones themselves from a bullet fired from those same slabs.

ON THE night of Friday June 9, Deng Xiaoping emerged after a 21-day absence. With his Mao-suited Politburo, Wan Li, and a clique of old cronies — but without Zhao — he appeared on television to praise the army commanders for crushing the "rebellion". The People's Liberation Army had proved to be China's "Great Wall of iron and steel," he said. The trouble, he declared, had been started by "a very small number of people" whose aim was to "overthrow the Communist Party and the socialist system. They wanted to transform the People's Republic of China into a bourgeois republic." In China, Deng's "very small number of people" could encompass thousands.

As the round-up began, the first publicized arrests were of minor "hooligans": sullen young men accused of arson, damage to public property and other crimes, who were shown on television handcuffed and being marched to interrogation cells. Four hundred "criminals" had been arrested by the end of the week.

An exemplary dissident was sought: Fang Lizhi, the astrophysicist and human rights activist, together with his wife, Li Shuxian. They were branded as "behind-the-scenes" instigators of the counter-revolution. Fortunately for them, they had taken refuge in the United States embassy the day after the army moved into Tiananmen Square. China demanded that Washington hand them over; the demand was rejected. Warrants were issued for their arrest, and frontier police alerted.

Next, it was the turn of the student commanders. A "most-wanted" list of 21 names and photographs was issued on June 13, including commentaries on physical appearance, background, birthplace and accent. The public was ordered to hunt them down and turn them in. The roll was headed by Wang Dan, Wuerkaixi, Liu Gang, and Chai Ling.

Wuerkaixi fled the country; Chai Ling disappeared. But by mid-August, seven of the 21, including Wang Dan and Liu Gang, were known to have been arrested. So too was Ren Wanding, the Democracy Wall veteran: nobody would hide him.

In the weeks which followed, the authorities announced the arrest of over 2,000 people across China. Human rights groups estimated the true figure to be at least five times as high. In Peking on June 17, eight people were sentenced to death for "rioting". They were peasants, unemployed workers, vagrants and "escaped criminals," whose specific crime had been to set fire to six vehicles in the early days of Martial Law. On June 21, three men who had set fire to a train in Shanghai were executed. The announcements of death sentences stopped towards the end of June, when the leadership decided that they were becoming counter-productive to the official claim that conditions in China had returned to normal.

On June 19, Li Peng, the prime minister, appeared on television in the company of his two allies on the Politburo Standing Committee, Qiao Shi and Yao Yilin. He announced that the "counter-revolution" was "basically over", and that the situation was "heading for stability." On June 23, *People's Daily* announced that a "decisive" victory had now been achieved. This confidence reflected developments within Zhongnanhai, rather than on the streets of Peking. The next day, three weeks after the attack on Tiananmen, it was announced that the Central Committee had been in session, and that it had made certain dispositions within the leadership. Zhao Ziyang, general secretary of the Communist Party, was relieved of his posts, and his supporters fell with him. A new Politburo Standing Committee was appointed, without Hu Qili; and Jiang Zemin, the Party boss from Shanghai, became Zhao's successor. For now at least, the old men had won.

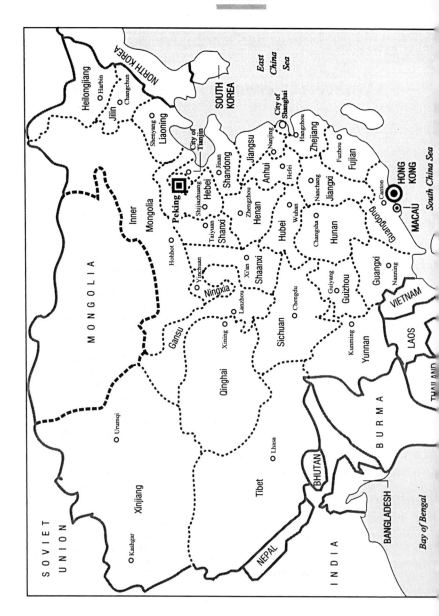

Contemporary events in selected provinces

Guangdong. On the evening of May 4, police tried unsuccessfully to halt a demonstration in Canton by thousands of students from Zhongshan University, Jinan University and Huannan Teacher's University. On May 16, another street procession was staged. The next day, a sit-in and 24-hour hunger strike was launched in front of the headquarters of the provincial government. By May 18, the crowd had swelled to 30,000. On June 4, students occupied the Haizhou Bridge in Canton for one hour. The next day, they returned to block traffic at so many key locations as to bring the city to a standstill, and paralyzed the railway system by lying on the tracks at Tianhe District. On June 6, 19 "hooligans" were briefly arrested. The provincial government announced new regulations against unofficial bodies, and set up a special discipline and inspection unit for colleges. By June 27, students had returned to class.

Hubei. The seriousness of events in Hubei could be judged from a notice which appeared after order had been restored. It threatened action against ringleaders who had been "collecting crowds to storm party and government organs and factories, mines and enterprises, and to block traffic and disrupt social order, resulting in the cutting of road and railway traffic, and criminal elements who took part in smashing, looting and burning. "Over half" the city's students were officially regarded as having been involved in the unrest.

On April 28, the province's deputy party secretary urged a "clear-cut stand" against disorder. On May 16, students began a sit-in at one end of a bridge over the Yangtze River at Wuhan, bringing heavy traffic to a standstill. On May 22, the city was placed under control of the military police. They used pepper, tear gas and cattle prods to disperse crowds. Deng was widely rumoured to be in the city at this time.

On June 4, students staged a sit-in to block tracks on Wuchang bridge. In the following week, police began arresting activists. On June 7, they reported detaining "criminal elements." On June 10, the public security bureau said it had arrested 28 "unemployed and disreputable workers" who had been shouting slogans and harassing passers-by. On June 11, most students returned to their classes. On June 15, the Wuhan College Students' Autonomous Federation was officially banned. Newspapers were advised to "improve their management."

Hunan. Hunan was Hu Yaobang's home province. The response to his death was severe. As early as April 22, incidents of beating, smashing and looting were reported on the streets of Changsha. Nine people were arrested in connection with this riot a week later. On May 4, about 2,000 students demonstrated. On May 17, many times that number came together to support the Peking hunger strike. About 10,000 congregated at the main railway station. Tens of thousands more students, teachers, journalists and blue-collar workers took to the streets the next day.

Rallies of this magnitude continued for at least another week, focused on a sit-in outside the provincial government headquarters which lasted until May 29. On May 23, four foreign teachers said that they saw more than 40 students and workers being beaten up at the bridge by at least three truckloads of soldiers. After the Peking massacre, protestors brought the city to a standstill. The chaos lasted at least until June 9, when the mayor of Changsha appealed for order. Two days later, the public security bureau had arrested at least 31 "rioters." On June 15, police searched nine publishing houses believed to have printed "counter-revolutionary" material.

Shaanxi. Residents of Xian gathered to mourn Hu Yaobang on April 19. On April 22, the day of his funeral, riots broke out. Ten vehicles and twenty houses were burnt. At Xincheng Square, 130 armed police were reported injured. Police trucks invested the town. On April 26, police said they were making arrests. Students at the Northwestern Industrial University received permission to demonstrate on the streets on May 4. On May 17, they petitioned for a meeting with the governor, and began a hunger-strike, calling for the "truth" about the April 22 disturbance to be "clarified."

On May 20, Xian was brought to a standstill as 300,000 protestors took to the streets. Students occupied the central square, and showed pictures which they said illustrated police brutality on April 22. Demonstrations continued in the square until May 28, when students returned to school. On June 3, three Americans were expelled, accused of impersonating students.

On June 10-11, the provincial Party issued a series of orders. It banned autonomous workers' and students' unions, and the production of "reactionary slogans." On June 12, 43 "saboteurs" were arrested; on June 13, 75 "lawbreakers", including student leaders.

Shanghai. The first reported demonstration took place in the early hours of April 20, five days after Hu's death. Several hundred students marched to the municipal government headquarters on Waitan — the Bund — and were later joined by large crowds of onlookers. The city's Party boss, Jiang Zemin, complained on April 26 about the appearance of big character posters around university campuses. The first large daytime demonstration took place on May 2, when 6,000 students marched from their colleges to People's Square in the centre of the city. On May 4, about 5,000 students marched again to People's Square, where they began a sit-in outside the municipal government headquarters; on May 16, 4,000 students and young teachers decided to stage their own hunger-strike in sympathy with Peking. On May 17-18 the protests multiplied in size to embrace all sectors of the society. Cadres paraded alongside students and workers. On May 20, two days after Mikhail Gorbachev's stopover, the students placed a small model of the Statue of Liberty outside the government headquarters, which probably served as the inspiration for the more dramatic "Goddess of Democracy," produced by the Central Institute of Fine Art for erection on Tiananmen Square a week later.

A mass march on May 28 march signalled the onset of worse disruption, reaching near-chaos after the June 3-4 Peking massacre. Crowds sat-in on railway tracks leading into the city centre, and on June 6 demonstrators blocking the line at Guangxin junction were mown down by a train. At least six were killed, and as many again injured. The crowd set fire to the train. By now, the official crackdown was underway. On June 9, nine members of the Autonomous Workers' Union were arrested. On June 10, the municipal police said they had uncovered two "counter-revolutionary cliques", the China Youth Democratic Party and the Freedom Society, and repeated their declaration that unofficial student organizations were illegal. That same day, the police made ten arrests in connection with the June 6 assault on the train. The next day, they detained a Hong Kong student, Yao Yongzhan, accusing him of being involved with illegal activities, and expelled a British journalist, Peter Newport.

The arrests of "ruffians" and "criminals" accelerated. By June 13, 166 had been reported. On June 15, three of those arrested for firing the train were sentenced to death — the first publicized use of the death penalty in connection with the democracy movement. On June 21, the executions were carried out.

Sichuan. On April 19, "many people" were said to be mourning Hu Yaobang, who had close ties with Sichuan; it was also Deng's home province, and the province governed by Zhao until 1980. On April 20, students demonstrated in the centre of Chengdu. The next day, they staged a memorial service for Hu on Renmin Nanlu Square. Sporadic demonstrations continued, focused on a sit-in on the square. On May 17, the provincial vice-governor agreed to meet students the following day. Many students were trying to board trains to Peking. By June 1, protestors were blockading main roads around Chengdu. One was killed and five injured, when a goods vehicle crashed into a blockade.

On June 4, Chengdu's main department store was burnt down. Radio reports said the crowd also burnt a police station and fire engines which tried to intervene. Police were attacked with stones and bottles. The next day saw further intense violence. A Japanese visitor claimed that 300 students were killed, and a thousand injured. An attempt was made to burn the Jinjiang Hotel, which housed the US consulate. On June 6, further disturbances were reported; and also 100 arrests.

The authorities were beginning to crack down. On June 10, "criminals" were called upon to surrender. On June 14, autonomous organizations were banned. Chengdu police made 106 arrests on June 19; and on July 18, two "counter-revolutionaries" were executed.

Index

146